QUILT TRADITIONS

DEVON LAVIGNE

12 Striking Projects, 9 Skill-Building Techniques

KANSAS CITY
STAR QUILTS

Text copyright © 2017 by Devon Lavigne

Photography and artwork copyright © 2017 by C&T Publishing, Inc.,

Publisher: Amy Marson

Creative Director: Gailen Runge

Editors: Liz Aneloski and Donna di Natale

Technical Editor: Debbie Rodgers

Cover Designer: Page + Pixel

Book Designer: Kerry Graham

Production Coordinator: Joe Edge

Production Editor: Alice Mace Nakanishi

Illustrator: Aliza Shalit

Photo Assistants: Carly Jean Marin and Mai Yong Vang

Hand Model: Kristi Visser

Photography by Diane Pedersen of C&T Publishing, unless otherwise noted

Published by Kansas City Star Quilts, an imprint of C&T Publishing, Inc.,
P.O. Box 1456, Lafayette, CA 94549

Library of Congress Cataloging-in-Publication Data

Names: Lavigne, Devon, 1969- author.

Title: Quilt traditions : 12 striking projects, 9 skill-building techniques /
Devon Lavigne.

Description: Lafayette, CA : C&T Publishing, Inc., 2017. | Includes
bibliographical references.

Identifiers: LCCN 2016045932 | ISBN 9781617455223 (soft cover)

Subjects: LCSH: Patchwork--Patterns. | Quilting--Patterns.

Classification: LCC TT835 .L378 2017 | DDC 746.46--dc23

LC record available at https://lccn.loc.gov/2016045932

Printed in the USA

10 9 8 7 6 5 4 3 2 1

Dedication

My own quilting has been inspired over the past twenty years by authors, teachers, designers, and regular folks, whose passion and enthusiasm for the art of quilting shows in the remarkable pieces they create. I wrote this, in part, for the quilters who came before me.

And for my precious kids, whose ordinary, beautiful lives inspire me everyday. I love you, Meg, Abbey, Matt, and Ally.

And mostly for Rob, my life and my best friend. I love you.

Acknowledgments

Thank you to my mother, Louise Cutforth, for always being game to piece for me. This time she got stuck with the 145 blocks of *Thrift Shop Junkie* (page 68). Her patient support and goodwill inspire me to be a better mother, wife, and person.

Thank you also to Sharon Blackmore of Love Shack Quilts. Sharon's my girl: She's a fierce *artiste* and a gifted quilt and longarm quilting designer. I don't think longarm quilting has been discussed much yet as an art form, but there are those who truly are artists of longarm quilting—a bit like tattoo artists—and Sharon's one. Sharon hosts mystery quilts on Facebook with Prairie Quilt Militia, and together with her husband, Jason, she has created online quilting games. Check out Sharon's longarm designs and Prairie Quilt Militia (loveshackquilts.com) and their online games (unlocktheblock.ca).

And thanks to Kim Jamieson-Hirst, who is a gifted quilter and educator. She creates designs for quilts, soft toys, and hand embroidery under the name Chatterbox Quilts (chatterboxquilts.com), supervised by her "purry" assistants, Charlie and Teeka. Kim enjoys sharing information about quilting, vintage sewing machines, and other fabric-y goodness through her online courses and YouTube videos. Contact Kim at kim@chatterboxquilts.com.

CONTENTS

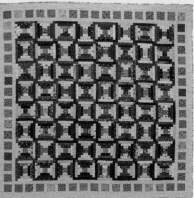

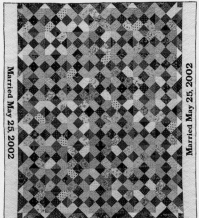

INTRODUCTION

I have three girls, currently between ages 16 and 23, and one long-suffering boy, currently 19. I smile to myself when I hear them talk about their favorite television show or the book everyone's reading, not to mention their own "he said, she said" experiences. My girls get right into that story—whatever it is—they really care about the characters' lives.

The same applies to art in all its forms; it's meant to engage us. To make us care. That's why a good quilt design offers both a design and a concept behind it. It's an invitation for the quilter to embrace the quilt as a story from his or her own life. For example, *Twenty-Five* (page 74)—full of promise and rent days—reminds us what it's like to be that tender age. *Little Black Dress* (page 36) is a nod to the famous accoutrement every girl's closet should hold. And *The Oath* (page 63) has a wide, snowy-white border that can be used to display appliquéd or embroidered dates and remembrances of life events such as service dates, marriages, and anniversaries.

I've tried to design a series of quilts that I hope most people can engage with, find similarities to their own experience in, or make personal to themselves. In some cases the story was informed by the emerging design, and sometimes the story "wrote" the quilt. *The Mister* (page 58) made his appearance when I was struggling with another design, so I went with him!

I hope quilters will find engaging designs and a bit of useful knowledge in *Kiss Me* (page 27). I've used techniques such as paper piecing, partial seams, and templates, but I hope I've translated tricky methods into easy-to-understand lessons, just as I learned them.

—*Devon*

NOTES

Tips

This section is not meant to be a comprehensive how-to, merely a collection of tips that I've learned over the years from excellent teachers, through repetition, or through trial and error (a lot of trial and error).

Books like Carrie and Harriet Hargrave's Quilter's Academy series (by C&T Publishing) are excellent new references and very thorough. Harriet is known for piecing precision and great use of simple tools.

One of my favorite reference books from the early 1990s, when first I started quilting, is *Great Quiltmaking: All the Basics* (by Better Homes and Gardens). I find the text easy to understand, and the illustrations are helpful. I still refer to my copy on occasion. No doubt there are many great reference sources—choose one to have on hand. Your local quilt shop will have one to recommend.

¼˝ SEAM ALLOWANCE

Unfortunately, not all ¼˝ machine presser feet are accurate. If you have trouble sewing an accurate ¼˝ seam, a piece of masking tape can solve that problem. Place a clear ruler under your machine's presser foot and gently lower the needle by hand until the needle touches the ruler at exactly the ¼˝ mark. Place a piece of masking tape to the right of the ruler, as shown in the photo. The masking tape is now a guide for the edge of the fabric.

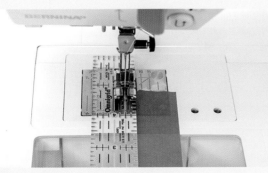

Mark the ¼˝ seam, using masking tape.

SCANT ¼˝ SEAMS

A scant ¼˝ is about a thread's width narrower than an exact ¼˝. It doesn't seem like much, but a thread's width allows for the fold of the fabric over the seam, and on blocks with a lot of seams, it can really mean the difference between a block that finishes to the correct size and one that doesn't.

SQUARING BLOCKS

Squaring the blocks, or elements within the block, is the key to a perfect quilt top.

1. Position a square ruler on the top of the block. It's easiest to use a ruler that is just a bit larger than the block, and not too big. Be sure the block is at least the size it should be or that there is excess fabric extending beyond the specified block size. Trim away the excess fabric on top and right side of block.

2. Turn the block 180°, lining up the specified block size on the ruler with what is now the freshly cut bottom and left side of the block. Again trim away the excess fabric on top and right side of block.

NOTE

Always be aware that trimming away too much can result in cutting away triangle points and other elements, so be very careful. It's better to stitch with an accurate scant seam allowance than to have to trim.

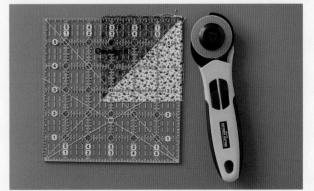

Square the blocks.

BIAS-JOINED SEAMS

1. Press the strips and lay them right side up on the cutting board. (You can cut several at once.) Locate the 45° angle on the ruler, and position this on the bottom edge of the strips. Cut to make a 45° angle.

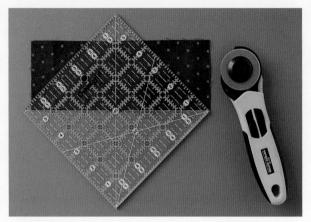

Cut a 45° angle.

TIP

Try using a starch alternative, such as Mary Ellen's Best Press, to limit stretching of the bias edges. Best Press makes the fabric more manageable by slightly stiffening it, like the starch widely used in the past, but without leaving a residue. Not only does it make pressing easier but it makes cutting more accurate. I use it sparingly. Sometimes I lightly spray a stack of patches and let them sit in a stack for a few minutes. Pressing is then easy!

2. Trim ¼″ off the points of the strips left by the 45° cut. This is an important step—it helps you to precisely place the next piece to be stitched. There are great point trimmers available for just this purpose, or simply use any ruler to measure the ¼″ point and trim.

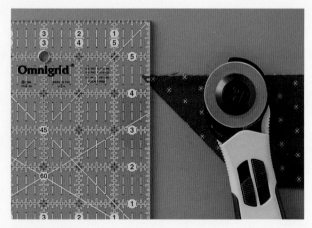

Trim the points.

3. To join 2 strips together, lay the first strip on the cutting board, right side up. Lay the second strip right side down and at a 90° angle to the first strip. Stitch, using a ¼″ seam, being careful not to stretch the bias.

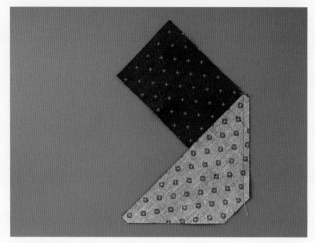

Join the strips.

4. Press the seam open.

Techniques

WORKING WITH TEMPLATES
TIP

I keep an old rotary cutter for template making. Likely it was used at one time by a family member for something other than cutting fabric. It may be useless for fabric, but it is still great for paper.

I used to avoid templates, thinking they were too difficult to work with. Some blocks, though, are just easier to make either paper pieced or with templates. And the truth is, I learned that templates are *easy* to work with—but they do take some preparation. The projects *Kiss Me* (page 27), *Little Black Dress* (page 36), and *Twenty-Five* (page 74) are all made with templates.

There are a lot of great products on the market for making templates, but the supplies for the method I use can be found in a kindergarten classroom: paper, scissors, a glue stick, and cardboard. The kind of cardboard from a shipping box with the corrugated middle is best, because it's thicker than the cardboard from a cereal box, for example. The extra thickness works perfectly for template use. I even carefully cut around round edges with my rotary cutter.

1. Photocopy or print the pattern.

2. Rough-cut around the pattern piece about ¼″ outside the dashed line.

3. Glue the pattern to the cardboard.

4. Cut out the template on the outer line. For straight edges, use the straight edge of the ruler; for round edges, practice (carefully) freehand cutting with the rotary cutter. If you use a ruler to hold down the part of the template you're not cutting, you can keep your hand out of the way—always a good idea! If that method seems uncomfortable, use sharp scissors to cut the curves.

Rotary cut around the template.

Marking the Fabric

TIP

One way to make working with templates a breeze is to use a starch alternative. By slightly stiffening the fabric, a starch alternative makes tricky maneuvers such as set-in seams much easier to execute. It's possible to use too much—a light spritz before the first press is sufficient.

The most important thing to remember about using directional templates or other directional pieces (as in *Mad Housewife*, page 42, and *The Mister*, page 58) is to be careful about fabric direction. When cutting basic shapes such as squares and rectangles for a traditional block, most people simply cut the fabric back to back, the way it comes off the bolt. This procedure isn't recommended when using directional templates because half the fabric pieces will be mirrored.

The easiest way to remedy this problem while still cutting efficiently is to use fat quarters. Press them and lay them right side up in layers. I work with only two layers, three if I have a really sharp blade.

If using yardage, cut off approximately half a yard of the still-folded fabric to work with. Cut the fabric in half down the fold, wasting as little as possible. Then switch the direction of one piece so both are layered right side up.

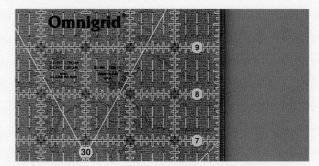

Cut off the fold.

1. Lay the cardboard template on the wrong side of the fabric and mark all around the template.

2. Cut out the fabric pieces on the marked line.

NOTE

It's very important to precisely cut even the small corners on the ends of the templates, because they show fabric placement when stitching the pieces together. Round or intricate edges will have to be cut with scissors.

3. If the pieces include a seam allowance, use the ¼″ mark on the ruler to draw a seamline ¼″ inside the marked line of each fabric piece. I actually only mark the corners, knowing that my ¼″ presser foot will be accurate on the straight edges. If the pattern has set-in seams, as in *Kiss Me* (page 27), it's important to mark corners so you know exactly where to stop and start stitching, which is the key to beautiful set-in seams.

Draw around the template and mark the corners.

The pieces are now ready to be stitched together, according to the pattern.

SET-IN SEAMS

A set-in seam is one that is set into an inside corner. Stars and other diamond-shaped pieces typically require set-in seams. The reason it's important to mark the seamline, or at least the corners, when working with templates is that the stitching starts and stops exactly at the marked corner in order to keep the seam allowance free to be stitched to both inside seams.

To Set-In a Seam

1. Press the 2 pieces, ideally using a starch alternative. It makes the stitching much easier.

2. Place the pieces to be set-in, right sides together, matching the marked corner of the top piece with the corner of the pieces below. Pin.

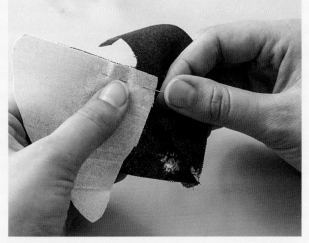

Pin set-in seams.

3. Starting at one end, stitch to the corner mark. Try to be very precise. The finished seam will be perfect if the stitching ends right at the corner mark. Backstitch 1 or 2 stitches to secure.

NOTE

I don't usually secure seams with a back-stitch in quilting, but in this case it's a good idea, as the corner will be handled a bit when stitching the adjacent seam.

4. Match the seam of the adjacent piece with adjacent corner mark. This may take some adjusting, but as you learn how to handle the fabric, it will get easier.

5. Starting at one end, stitch to the corner mark. Take 1 or 2 backstitches to secure.

Stitch the adjacent corner.

6. Press as indicated in the pattern. In star blocks, where this method is frequently used, the seams are usually pressed toward the star.

CURVED PIECING

Seams that are rounded or circular require curved piecing. It looks much more difficult than it is. The trick is to mark the centers of the blocks or elements, by folding them in half to find the center or using the center seams, and then pin them in place, matching the center folds or seams.

Pinning (a lot of pinning) is your best friend when piecing curves.

Curved piecing

PAPER PIECING

I like paper (foundation) piecing because it's so accurate. For blocks that have very tiny pieces or odd shapes, paper piecing is very helpful. I used paper piecing for the blocks in *Little Black Dress* (page 36).

Precut the Fabrics

Unfortunately, paper piecing does require more fabric than traditional piecing, but precutting the fabric can make more economical use of it. For *Little Black Dress*, the instructions say that some of the black and blue fabrics should be cut to roughly 2½″ × 6½″ and that some of the neutral fabrics should be roughly cut to 3″ × 3″. Precutting will result in less waste.

The designer of a paper-pieced quilt will provide a block pattern that can be copied or printed as many times for as many blocks as you need. Make sure the prints or copies are the same size as the original. It's essential to do a test copy (or several!) to arrive as close as possible to the indicated block size. For instance, the Little Black Dress block is supposed to be 8½″ × 8½″ square, but I found the copy I made to be a tiny fraction of an inch off in both directions. I aimed to come as close to 8½″ square as possible.

NOTE

There are lovely papers on the market that can be used for paper piecing, but I just use the paper provided by my copy shop (standard photocopy paper). I find I still need to rip out a seam every so often, and copy paper is sturdy enough to stand up to my "oops." Try a few different papers to see which you prefer.

Cut Apart Pattern Sections

Once you've copied the block pattern, you may need to cut the pattern into sections. One section is stitched at a time, and then the sections are joined. *Little Black Dress* has four sections that are marked for joining by *dashed lines* on the outside edges. Using scissors or a rotary cutter, rough-cut around these dashed lines.

TIP

You'll be stitching the fabric onto these paper sections, so before beginning to stitch, make sure to have a new, sharp needle.

Begin Stitching Sections 1 and 2

It is important that you follow the order of the pieces within each section. Each section will likely be marked A1, A2, A3, and then B1, B2, B3, and so on. The pattern will tell you which fabrics to use for each segment.

1. Begin by placing the fabrics for pieces 1 and 2 right sides together, with the piece 1 fabric on top. Pin the pattern right side up on top of the fabrics, making sure the fabric pieces are at least ¼″ larger than the sections to be covered.

2. Set the stitch length to shorter than normal to allow for tearing the paper off at the end. (I use 1.8 or 2.0 on my machine.) Sew on the line between sections 1 and 2. Start and end a couple stitches beyond the line so that each seam will be slightly overlapped by the next seam.

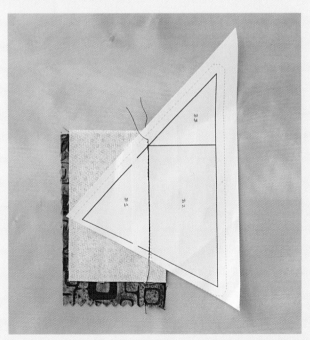

Stitch fabrics 1 and 2.

Until you're comfortable with how this process works, do some testing. When the seam is opened, does the fabric cover both sections 1 and 2 by at least ¼˝ past the dashed lines on all sides?

After all the stitching is completed, the paper pattern needs to be torn from the back of the block. The smaller stitch length will protect the seams.

Don't skimp on the seam allowance. Removing the paper pattern puts stress on a seam, and anything less than ¼˝ is not sturdy enough to withstand the strain.

Trimming the Seam

It's important to trim the seam to reduce the bulk from many layers of fabric.

1. Fold the paper back on the stitched line. Using a small ruler and rotary cutter, trim the seam to ¼˝. Just as in traditional piecing, the ¼˝ seam is king.

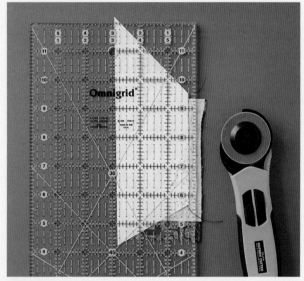

Trim the seam to ¼˝.

I keep a small rotary cutter handy on my cutting board, as well as a 6˝ × 12˝ ruler. I find these are the perfect size for the job, and they don't get in my way when I'm not using them.

2. Open the fabrics and press the seam toward piece 2. Make sure the paper is flat on the back of the fabrics when you press.

Stitching the Next Section

1. Choose the fabric for piece 3 and lay it on piece 2, right sides together. Check to make sure it will extend ¼˝ outside all edges of section 3.

2. Stitch on the line between pieces 2 and 3, again starting and ending a couple of stitches beyond the line.

3. Open the fabrics and press the seam toward piece 3.

4. Continue until each section is complete.

5. Press a final time and trim all around on the dashed line. *Do not cut on the solid line—this is the seam allowance!*

6. Sew all the sections.

Finishing the Block

1. Join the sections in order (usually determined by number), pinning them right sides together and stitching on the solid line.

2. Press as directed.

MEASURING AND CUTTING PLAIN BORDERS

1. Trim the selvages off each end of the border strips.

2. Referring to Bias-Joined Seams (page 8), stitch the strips together to make one continuous strip.

3. Measure the length of the quilt through the center and sides. Average the three measurements and cut 2 border pieces to this size from the continuous strip.

Averaging the three measurements, even if there is only ¼˝ or so difference, will help make the quilt square.

4. Sew a border to each side of the quilt. Press seams toward the border.

5. Measure the width of the quilt through the center and at the top and bottom. Average the three measurements. Cut 2 pieces to this length from the remaining border strip and sew to the top and bottom. Press seams toward the border.

FINISHED BLOCK: 7½″ × 7½″

FINISHED QUILT: 54″ × 54″

LEVEL: Beginner+

BÉBÉ À LA MODE

Bébé à la Mode *means "trendy baby." Make this sweet quilt for your own little trendsetter in sea-foam green and dark pinks. This looks like tricky curved piecing, but it's just fused appliqué with pretty stitching. I used very soft neutral fabrics in the background to help the pink fabrics and topstitching really pop.*

MATERIALS

Assorted sea-foam green prints: 4 fat quarters (1 yard total) for blocks and border 2

Assorted neutral prints: 8 fat quarters (2 yards total) for blocks

Assorted dark pink prints: 4 fat quarters (1 yard total) for blocks

Dark pink print: ⅜ yard for border 1

Sea-foam green print: ½ yard for binding

Light neutral print: 1 yard for borders 2 and 3

Backing: 3½ yards

Batting: 60″ × 60″

Double-sided fusible web: 12 sheets 9″ × 12″ each (I use Steam-A-Seam.)

CUTTING

Use *Bébé à la Mode* patterns D and E (below left) to make templates D and E. For information on making and using templates, review Working with Templates (page 8).

NOTE

Because this method uses fusible web, no seam allowance is included in the patterns. Cut on the solid line.

Assorted sea-foam green prints

• Cut 12 strips 1¾″ × 22″; subcut 144 A squares 1¾″ × 1¾″.

• Use template E to mark 72 pieces on fusible web. Remove paper backing and lay fusible web on back of sea-foam print. Press. Cut out shapes.

Assorted neutral prints

• Cut 18 strips 1¾″ × 22″; subcut 144 B rectangles 1¾″ × 3″.

• Cut 29 strips 3″ × 22″; subcut 144 C rectangles 3″ × 4¼″.

Assorted dark pink prints

• Use template D to mark 144 pieces on fusible web. Remove paper backing and lay fusible web on back of dark pink print. Press. Cut out shapes.

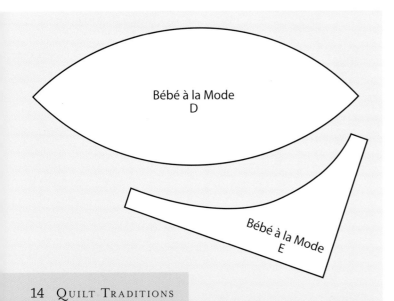

Dark pink print
- Cut 5 strips 1½″ × width of fabric for border 1.

Sea-foam green print
- Cut 6 strips 2¼″ × width of fabric for binding.

Light neutral print
- Cut 6 strips 2″ × width of fabric for border 2.
- Cut 6 strips 2½″ × width of fabric for border 3.

Construction

BLOCK ASSEMBLY

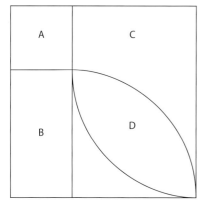

Block sketch

Making the Mini-Blocks

1. Stitch an A square to a B rectangle. Press the seam toward the A square.

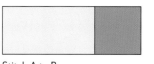

Stitch A to B.

2. Stitch a C rectangle to the A/B unit. Press the seam toward the C rectangle.

Stitch C to A/B.

3. Repeat Steps 1 and 2 to make 144 A/B/C mini-blocks.

ASSEMBLING THE BLOCK

1. Stitch the mini-blocks together in pairs. Press seam toward the left mini-block.

Mini-block pairs

2. Make 72 mini-block pairs.

3. Stitch a mini-block pair to a second mini-block pair. Make 36.

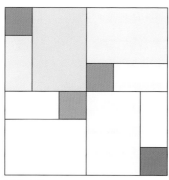

Make 36.

Appliquéing the D Pieces

1. Remove the paper backing and arrange 4 D pieces on each block with the points in the corners created by the A squares.

2. Press to fuse.

3. Finish the edges of the D pieces by machine or hand embroidery.

NOTE

I finished the edges of my pieces by machine, using dark pink coordinating thread.

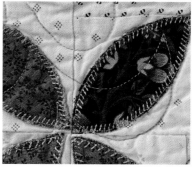

Machine appliqué the edges.

ASSEMBLING THE QUILT TOP

1. Referring to the quilt assembly diagram (page 16), stitch the blocks into 6 rows of 6 blocks each. Note the orientation of each block within the row. Do not press until each row is complete.

2. Press the seams in the odd rows (1, 3, and 5) to the right, and press the seams in the even rows (2, 4, and 6) to the left.

3. Sew the rows together, pinning the seams for accuracy. The seams should nestle nicely together.

4. Press all row seams in one direction, either up or down.

BORDERS 1, 2, AND 3

For attaching the borders, refer to Measuring and Cutting Plain Borders (page 12).

Appliquéing the E Pieces

1. Referring to the quilt assembly diagram, arrange the E pieces on border 2, using the seamlines between the borders and blocks as reference points.

2. Remove the paper backing and press in place.

3. Finish the edges by machine or hand stitching.

FINISHING

1. Cut the backing fabric in half to make 2 sections 40″ × 63″.

2. Cut off the selvages and stitch the sections together, along the 63″ edges using a ½″ seam allowance.

3. Layer, baste, quilt, and bind as desired.

Quilt assembly

FINISHED BLOCK: 9″ × 9″

FINISHED QUILT: 64″ × 76″

LEVEL: Intermediate

CLUB NIGHT

Dress up for late nights and disco lights in grays, bright whites, and cherry reds. I used a soft gray for the inner part of the quilt to give it a glow, and a darker, steelier gray for the outer pieces, including the setting triangles.

Sharon Blackmore of Love Shack Quilts, whose stunning quilting brings Club Night to life, describes the stitching as "two elements—circles and ribbons—grooving together in constant movement." Grooving, indeed!

Club Night is made up of two different blocks plus plain background blocks, for a total of 50 blocks.

As usual, I've chosen to make some elements of Club Night scrappy—the stars, in this case. For other elements, such as the background, I've used the same fabric throughout. That's why I've called for some fat quarters and some yardage. My advice is to go with yardage on areas that aren't scrappy. Yardage will go further than fat quarters because of the size of the blocks.

MATERIALS

Medium gray print 1: 2½ yards for blocks and setting triangles

Light gray print: 1½ yards for blocks

Gray floral print: ⅝ yard for blocks and corner triangles

Assorted red prints: 3 fat quarters (¾ yard total) for blocks

Assorted neutral prints: 3 fat quarters (¾ yard total) for blocks

Dark gray print: ⅝ yard for blocks

Cherry-red print: ⅜ yard for blocks

Light neutral print: ⅜ yard for blocks

Medium gray print 2: ⅝ yard for binding

Backing: 4¾ yards

Batting: 70″ × 82″

CUTTING

Medium gray print 1

- Cut 3 strips 9½" × width of fabric; subcut 12 squares 9½" × 9½" for background blocks.

- Cut 3 strips 14" × width of fabric; subcut 5 squares 14" × 14"; subcut twice diagonally to yield 18 setting triangles.

- Cut 4 strips 1½" × width of fabric; subcut 8 H strips 1½" × 7½" and 8 I strips 1½" × 9½" for the half-square blocks.

Light gray print

- Cut 3 strips 9½" × width of fabric; subcut 10 squares 9½" × 9½" for background blocks.

- Cut 4 strips 3⅞" × width of fabric; subcut 40 squares 3⅞" × 3⅞"; subcut once diagonally to yield 80 A triangles for star blocks.

- Cut 4 strips 1½" × width of fabric; subcut 8 H strips 1½" × 7½" and 8 I strips 1½" × 9½" for half-square blocks.

Gray floral print

- Cut 2 strips 3½" × width of fabric; subcut 20 E squares 3½" × 3½" for star blocks.

- Cut 1 strip 7¼" × width of fabric; subcut 2 squares 7¼" × 7¼"; subcut once diagonally to yield 4 corner triangles.

Assorted red prints

- Cut 8 strips 3⅞" × 22"; subcut 40 squares 3⅞" × 3⅞"; subcut once diagonally to yield 80 C triangles for star blocks.

Assorted neutral prints

- Cut 8 strips 3⅞" × 22"; subcut 40 squares 3⅞" × 3⅞"; subcut once diagonally to yield 80 D triangles for star blocks.

Dark gray print

- Cut 4 strips 3⅞" × width of fabric; subcut 40 squares 3⅞" × 3⅞"; subcut once diagonally to yield 80 B triangles for star blocks.

Cherry-red print

- Cut 1 strip 7⅞" × width of fabric; subcut 4 squares 7⅞" × 7⅞"; subcut once diagonally to yield 8 F triangles for half-square blocks.

Light neutral print

- Cut 1 strip 7⅞" × width of fabric; subcut 4 squares 7⅞" × 7⅞"; subcut once diagonally to yield 8 G triangles for half-square blocks.

Medium gray print 2

- Cut 8 strips 2¼" × width of fabric for binding.

Construction

MAKING THE STAR BLOCK

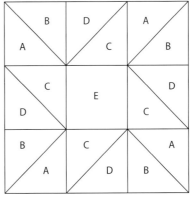

Star block sketch

Making the Half-Square Triangles

1. Stitch a light gray A triangle to a dark gray B triangle to make a half-square triangle. Press toward the B triangle.

2. Repeat Step 1 to make 80 A/B half-square triangles.

3. Repeat Step 1 with the assorted red C triangles and the assorted neutral D triangles to make 80 C/D half-squares. Press toward the red C triangles.

4. Square the half-square triangle blocks to 3½".

Finishing the Star Block

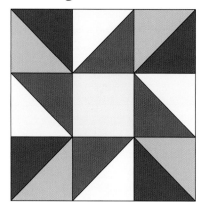

Star block

1. Lay out 4 A/B half-square triangles, 4 C/D half-square triangles, and a center E square, according to the star block diagram.

2. Noting the orientation of the half-square triangles, stitch an A/B half-square triangle on each side of a C/D half-square triangle to create an end unit. Press toward the C/D half-square triangles.

3. Repeat to make a second A/B end unit.

4. Stitch a C/D half-square triangle to each side of a E square to make a center unit. Press toward the E square.

5. Matching and pinning seams, stitch an end unit on each side of a center unit. Press seams in either direction.

MAKING THE HALF-SQUARE BLOCK

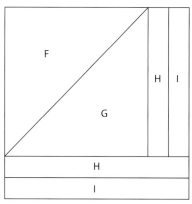

Half-square triangle block sketch

Making the Half-Square Triangles

1. Stitch an F triangle to G triangle to make a half-square triangle. Press toward the F triangle.

2. Repeat Step 1 to make 8 F/G half-square triangles.

3. Square the half-square triangles to 7½″.

Adding the H Strips

1. Stitch a light gray 1½″ × 7½″ H strip to a medium gray 1½″ × 7½″ H strip. Press in either direction.

2. Stitch this unit to an F/G half-square triangle along either of the G sides. Press toward the H strips.

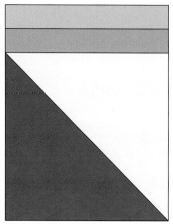

Add the H strips.

Adding the I Strips

1. Stitch a light gray 1½″ × 9½″ I strip to a medium gray 1½″ × 9½″ I strip. Press in either direction.

2. Stitch this unit to the F/G half-square triangle along the other G side. Press toward the I strips.

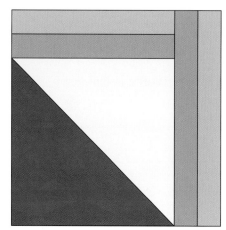

Add the I strips.

ASSEMBLING THE QUILT TOP

1. Referring to the quilt assembly diagram, arrange the star blocks, the half-square triangle blocks, the background blocks, and the setting triangles into rows. Note the orientation of each block within the row.

TIP

On-point designs, like this one, may seem difficult to lay out, but if you tilt the assembly illustration 45°, it's easy to see the design as a ten-row rectangle.

2. Stitch the blocks together into diagonal rows. Do not press until each row is complete. Press the seams in the odd rows (1, 3, 5, 7, and 9) to the right, and press the seams in the even rows (2, 4, 6, 8, and 10) to the left.

3. Join the rows together to make the quilt center, pinning the seams for accuracy. Because the odd row seams were pressed to the right and the even row seams to the left, the seams should nestle nicely together.

4. Press all row seams in one direction, either up or down.

FINISHING

1. Cut the backing fabric in half to make 2 sections 40″ × 85″.

2. Cut off the selvages and stitch the sections together along the 85″ side, using a ½″ seam allowance.

3. Layer, baste, quilt, and bind as desired.

Quilt assembly

Honeymoon

FINISHED BLOCK: 10″ × 10″

FINISHED QUILT: 100″ × 100″

LEVEL: Intermediate

With sparkling white beaches and a cool blue ocean, all you need is a mai tai for a perfect honeymoon vacation. I used blues, teals, and browns in all value ranges and tones. For the blocks, use strips from your scrap basket if you like, but you'll also need yardage—a nice, crisp light for the borders. And although I love fat quarters, this quilt doesn't lend itself to their best use, unless you make the biggest cuts first.

Honeymoon *is made up of 64 Courthouse Step blocks in an alternating layout.*

MATERIALS

Assorted light prints: 2⅞ yards for blocks

Assorted medium prints: 1⅝ yards for blocks and border 2

Assorted dark prints: 4 yards for blocks

Light yardage: 3½ yards for borders 1, 2, and 3 and binding

Backing: 3 yards of 108″-wide fabric

Batting: 106″ × 106″

CUTTING

I'm going to review 2 methods for piecing the Courthouse Step blocks, developed by Judy Martin. Method 1 is a very quick chain-piecing method, but make sure your ¼″ seam is exact. Log Cabin and Courthouse Step blocks cannot be squared down when the block is finished without distorting the last round. In Method 2, all the strips are cut ahead, which is not as quick but is very accurate.

Assorted light prints

- Cut 55 strips 1¾″ × width of fabric; *stop here if you've chosen Method 1.*

If you've chosen Method 2, subcut:

128 strips 1¾″ × 8″

128 strips 1¾″ × 5½″

128 strips 1¾″ × 3″

Assorted medium prints

- Cut 8 strips 4½″ × width of fabric; subcut 64 squares 4½″ × 4½″ for border 2.

- Cut 5 strips 3″ × width of fabric; subcut 64 squares 3″ × 3″.

Assorted dark prints

- Cut 79 strips 1¾″ × width of fabric; *stop here if you've chosen Method 1.*

  If you've chosen Method 2, subcut:

  128 strips 1¾″ × 10½″

  128 strips 1¾″ × 8″

  128 strips 1¾″ × 5½″

Light yardage

- Cut 15 strips 4½″ × width of fabric; set aside 11 strips for border 3 and subcut the other 4 strips into 64 rectangles 4½″ × 2″ for border 2.

- Cut 9 strips 2½″ × width of fabric for border 1.

- Cut 11 strips 2¼″ × width of fabric for binding.

Construction

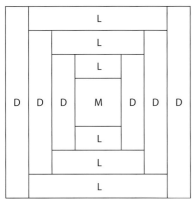

Honeymoon block sketch

If you've decided to make the Honeymoon blocks using Method 1, it's a good idea to make a practice block to ensure that the block finishes to 10½".

METHOD 1

1. Lay a light 1¾" strip right side up on your machine. Right sides together, stitch a medium 3" × 3" square to this strip.

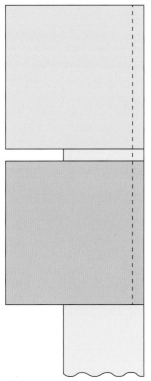

Chain piecing (Method 1)

2. Continue to sew medium squares to the light strip, leaving ¼" or so between the squares, until you reach the end of the light strip. Repeat until all 64 medium squares have been stitched to light strips.

TIP

This method can result in a less scrappy look if you don't mix up the medium squares when stitching them to the light strips. If you want to keep it scrappy, also make sure to mix up the fabrics so the medium squares are paired with various light strips.

3. Using a rotary cutter and ruler, trim between the medium squares. It's important to trim at exactly the edge of each medium square so that when opened and pressed, the light strips are the correct length (3" in this case).

Trim the medium squares after chain piecing (Method 1).

4. Press the seams to set and then press the seams open, using a starch alternative to keep the seams crisp.

5. Repeat Steps 1–4 to add light strips to the opposite side of the medium squares.

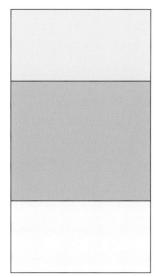

Sew light strips to the opposite sides of the medium squares (Method 1).

6. Repeat Steps 1–5 to add dark strips to the 2 remaining sides of the medium squares.

Sew dark strips to the medium squares.

Check Your Seams

This is a good time to test the accuracy of your seam allowance (see ¼˝ Seam Allowance, page 7). After the first row of "logs" is added, the block should measure 5½˝ × 5½˝ square. If not, adjust the seam allowance.

If the block is too large, the seam is a little to the left of an actual ¼˝. If the block is too small, the seam allowance is too far to the right of ¼˝.

7. Continue chain piecing until you have added 3 light strips and 3 dark strips to each side of all 64 medium squares.

METHOD 2

1. Pair a light 1¾˝ × 3˝ rectangle with a medium 3˝ × 3˝ square, right sides together. Sew together. Continue to chain piece light 1¾˝ × 3˝ rectangles to medium 3˝ squares.

Sew a light rectangle to a medium square (Method 2).

2. Separate the chains by trimming the threads between the units. Press to set the seams and then press the seams open, using a starch alternative to keep the seams crisp.

3. Repeat Steps 1 and 2 to add light rectangles to the opposite side of the medium squares.

4. In the same manner, add dark strips to the remaining to sides of the medium squares.

5. After the first row of "logs" is added, the block should measure 5½˝ × 5½˝.

6. Continue sewing, alternating light and dark strips, until you have added 3 sets of light strips and 3 sets of dark strips to each side of the medium square.

7. Make 64 Honeymoon blocks.

ASSEMBLING THE QUILT TOP

1. Referring to the quilt assembly diagram (page 26), arrange the blocks into 8 rows of 8 blocks each, alternating the orientation of every other block.

2. Join into rows, pinning if necessary.

I don't usually pin when joining blocks together, but I do find it necessary with blocks that can't be squared down, like these. It helps them ease into each other.

3. Press the joining seams of the odd rows (1, 3, 5, and 7) to the right, and press the joining seams of the even rows (2, 4, 6, and 8) to the left.

Border 1

Attach border 1, following the instructions in Measuring and Cutting Plain Borders (page 12).

Border 2

1. Make 2 pieced border strips by alternating 15 medium squares and 16 light border 2 rectangles, beginning and ending with the light rectangles. Press the seams toward the light rectangles.

2. Stitch a pieced border 2 to the top and bottom of the quilt. Press the seams toward border 1.

3. Make 2 pieced borders using 17 medium squares and 16 light rectangles, beginning and ending with the medium squares. Press the seams toward the light rectangles.

4. Stitch a pieced border to each side of the quilt. Press the seams toward border 1.

5. Stitch ⅛″ from the raw edge all the way around the entire border 2. This will keep the border from stretching when border 3 is added.

Border 3

Attach border 3, following the instructions in Measuring and Cutting Plain Borders (page 12).

FINISHING

Layer, baste, quilt, and bind as desired.

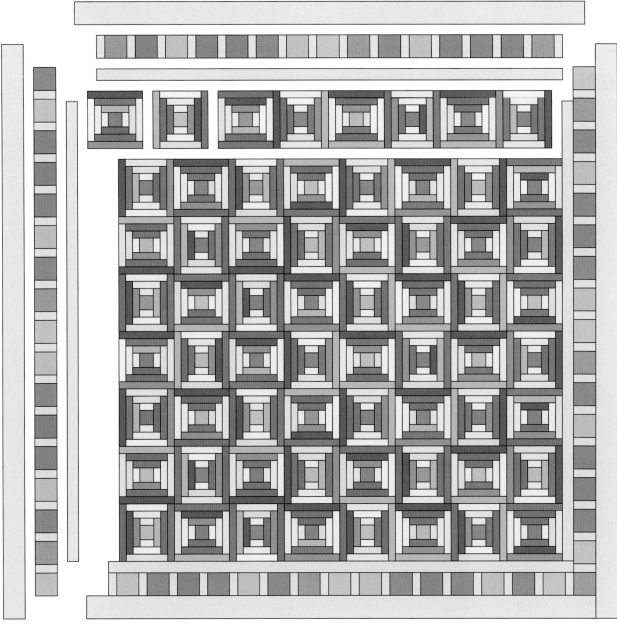

Quilt assembly

FINISHED BLOCKS: 20″ × 20″ | 10″ × 10″ | 5″ × 5″

FINISHED QUILT: 62″ × 80″

LEVEL: Intermediate/Advanced

Kiss Me

The sparkle of bubble-gum pink and cheery coral pair beautifully with romantic dove-gray florals—a perfect yin and yang. As my father-in-law likes to say, "It's a love story."

NOTE *Kiss Me* is a homage to *Wedding Bands*, a quilt designed by Judy Martin. I made it years ago, and it's still one my favorite quilts. The borders in this quilt are added by sewing partial seams. Partial seams are used when other, adjacent seams must be stitched first before completing the seam. Stitch only halfway, and then stop and remove the unit from the machine.

Kiss Me is made up of three block sizes. The tiny corner stars are 5˝, the medium stars are 10˝, and the feature star is 20˝, for a total of 43 blocks.

MATERIALS

Assorted bright bubble-gum pink/coral prints: 8 assorted fat quarters (2 yards total) for blocks

Dove-gray floral: 5½ yards for blocks and background

Coordinating gray floral print: 1¾ yards for blocks and background

Backing: 5 yards

Medium gray print: ⅝ yard for binding

Batting: 68˝ × 86˝

CUTTING

Use *Kiss Me* patterns A–I (pages 34 and 35) to make templates A–I. For information on making and using templates, review Working with Templates (page 8).

Assorted bright pink/coral prints
- Cut 8 with template A.
- Cut 240 with template D.
- Cut 96 with template G.

Dove-gray floral print
- Cut 2 strips 15½˝ × width of fabric; subcut 4 rectangles 15½˝ × 5½˝ for background blocks.

   From the remaining fabric:
   - Cut 8 with template B.
   - Cut 4 with template C.
   - Cut 208 with template E.
   - Cut 104 with template F.
   - Cut 96 with template H.
   - Cut 48 with template I.

Coordinating gray floral print
- Cut 3 strips 10½˝ × width of fabric; subcut 4 rectangles 10½˝ × 11½˝ and 8 rectangles 10½˝ × 5½˝ for background blocks.
- Cut 4 strips 1½˝ × width of fabric for side borders.
- Cut 32 with template E.
- Cut 16 with template F.

Medium gray print
- Cut 8 strips 2¼˝ × width of fabric for binding.

Construction

BLOCK ASSEMBLY

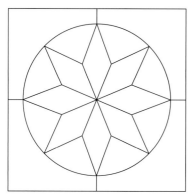

TIP

Start by piecing a 10˝ star, which will be easier to work with than the 5˝ minis. By the time you've put together 30 medium-size stars, you'll be a pro at the small stars. When you've tackled these, finish with the 20˝ star feature block.

Making the Star

Note that the diamond patterns (A, D, and G) have short and long sides—the shorter sides (labeled 1 on the pattern) are stitched together in the center.

1. Stitch 2 D pieces, right sides together, along the short side 1.

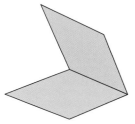

Stitch a D/D unit.

2. Press the seam toward the right D piece.

3. Repeat to make 4 D/D units.

Setting-in the Background Pieces

1. Sew an E piece into a D/D unit, referring to Set-In Seams (page 10). Press the seams toward the D pieces.

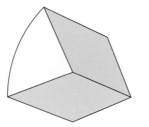

Sew E to D, using a set-in seam.

2. Repeat Step 1 to make 4 D/D pairs with an E piece set-in.

3. Stitch 2 D/E/D units together. Press the seam to the right.

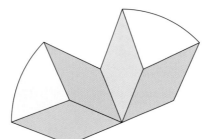

Stitch 2 D/E/D units together.

4. Sew an E piece into the D/E/D pair, using a set-in seam. Press the seams toward the D pieces.

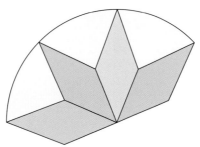

Sew an E piece to a D/D pair.

5. Repeat Steps 3 and 4 to make a second unit.

6. Match and pin the center seam, and then stitch the 2 star halves. Press the seams in either direction.

7. Finish by adding the remaining 2 E pieces. Press the seam toward the D pieces.

FINISHING THE BLOCK

1. Stitch 2 F pieces together along one short end, right sides together. Press the seam toward the right.

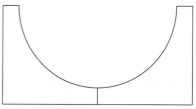

Stitch 2 F pieces together.

2. Repeat Step 1 to stitch the second set of F pieces.

3. Stitch the F/F pairs together at the remaining short ends. This will create the background circle for the star.

Fitting the Star into the Background

1. Lay the background circle flat on your cutting board. Place the star inside, matching up the 4 F seams to a star seam. There is no particular direction for the star.

2. Pin the star to the inside edge of the background, matching seams, and finger-press the F seams opposite the star seams.

It will seem as if there's too much fabric in the background to fit the star, but it does fit. Match the 4 background seams to the star seams first, and then pin the remaining star seams at the midpoint between the background seams. Pin several times between the midpoint seams.

3. Stitch carefully, with the background fabric on the bottom and the star on top. The feed dogs on the machine will help ease in any excess fabric.

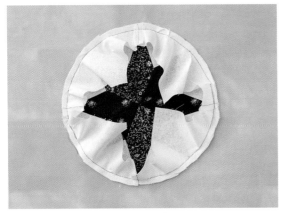

Fit the star into the background circle.

4. Spritz with a starch alternative. Press the seams toward the background. The block should measure 10½″ × 10½″.

5. Repeat the steps in Block Assembly (page 29) and Finishing the Block (page 29) to make 24 star blocks with a dove-gray background.

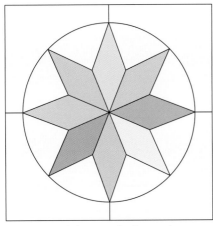

Star block with dove-gray background

6. Repeat the steps in Block Assembly and Finishing the Block to make 2 star blocks with a coordinating fabric background.

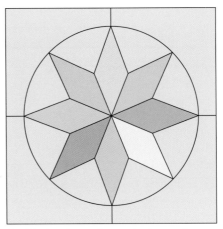

Star block with coordinating background

7. Repeat the steps in Block Assembly and Finishing the Block to make 4 star blocks using both backgrounds for half of each block.

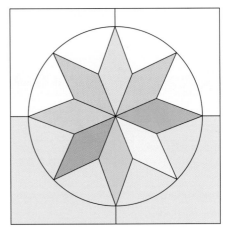

Star block with both backgrounds

MAKE THE REMAINING BLOCKS

1. Repeat the steps in Block Assembly and Finishing the Block to make 12 star blocks measuring 5″, using templates G, H, and I.

2. Repeat the steps in Block Assembly and Finishing the Block to make 1 feature 20″ star block, using templates A, B, and C.

ASSEMBLING THE QUILT TOP
Making the Groupings

1. Arrange the star blocks and background blocks according to the quilt assembly diagram (page 33).

2. Refer to the numbered groups for assembling the quilt top. Stitch the groups in numerical order.

NOTE

Because of the need to use partial seams when assembling the quilt top, there are special instructions for making the sections or groupings for the quilt top. Make groupings in the order recommended so that the partial seams work together.

GROUP 1

1. Stitch A to B. Press the seam toward A.

2. Stitch C to A/B, using a partial seam. Stop stitching the seam halfway through A. Finger-press the seam toward C. It will be completed when the side borders are added.

3. Stitch D to E. Press the seam toward E.

4. Stitch D/E to B/C. Press the seam toward B/C

5. Stitch F to G. Press the seam toward G.

6. Stitch A/B/D to F/G. Press the seam toward F/G.

7. Repeat Steps 1–6 to make 2 sections of Group 1 and 2 *mirrored* sections of Group 1.

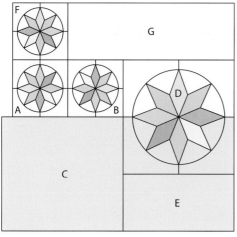

Group 1

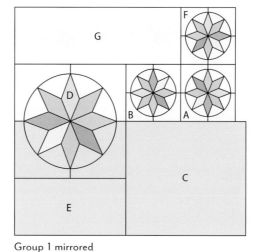

Group 1 mirrored

GROUP 2

1. *Seam 1:* Stitch A to B. Press the seam toward A.

2. *Seam 2:* Stitch B to C. Press the seam toward C.

3. *Seam 3:* Stitch D to E. Press the seam open.

4. *Seam 4:* Stitch A/B/C to D/E. Press the seam open.

5. Repeat Steps 1–4 to make 2 Group 2 sections.

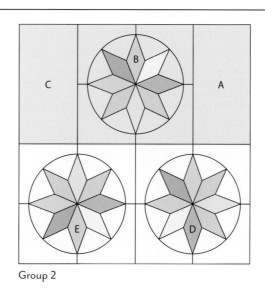

Group 2

GROUP 3

Stitch 12 of the 10″ star blocks into 2 rows of 6 stars each. Press the seams in either direction.

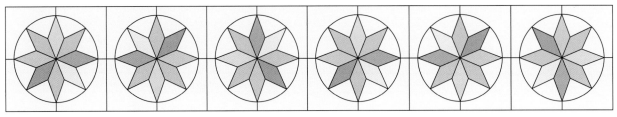

Group 3

GROUP 4

1. Stitch the remaining 10″ star blocks into pairs.

2. Join the pairs to make 2 sections of Group 4.

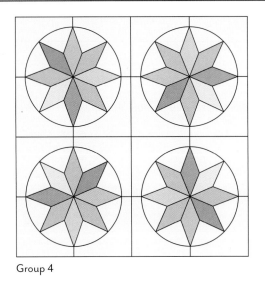

Group 4

Finishing the Center

1. Referring to the quilt assembly diagram (next page), pin and stitch a Group 1 section to each side of a Group 2 section, noting the orientation of each.

2. Repeat to make a second Group 1-2 section.

3. Stitch a Group 4 to each side of the 20″ feature star block. Press the seams toward the feature star block.

4. Stitch a Group 3 row to each side of the center section. Press the seams in either direction.

5. Stitch a Group 1-2 section to each side of the center section. Press the seam in either direction.

Side Borders

1. Referring to Bias-Joined Seams (page 8), stitch the side border strips together to make a continuous strip.

2. Cut into 2 strips 1½″ × 60½″.

3. Stitch 1 strip to 1 side of the quilt. Notice that the side border does not extend the whole length of the quilt. It starts and stops at the C block, which is the corner. Press the seam toward the border.

4. Repeat Step 3 to add the second strip to the opposite side.

5. Finish the partial seam between C and the side borders at all 4 corners. Press the seam toward C.

FINISHING

1. Cut the backing fabric in half to make 2 sections 40″ × 90″.

2. Cut off the selvages and stitch the sections together along a 90″ side, using a ½″ seam allowance.

3. Layer, baste, quilt, and bind as desired.

Quilt assembly

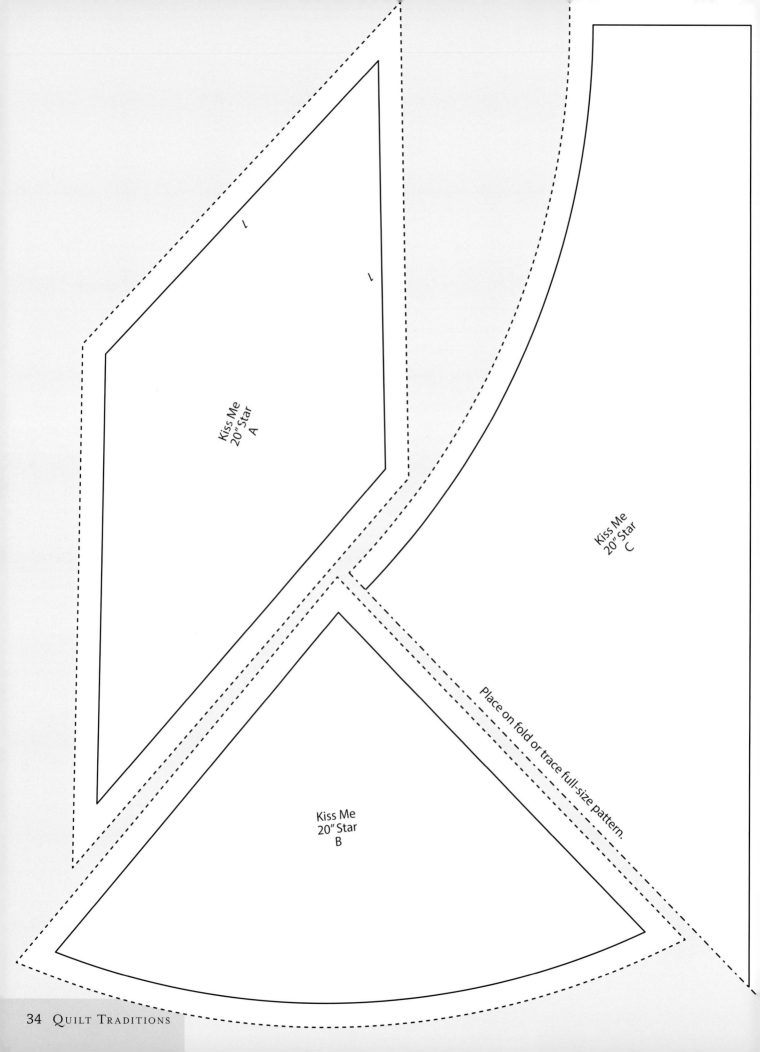

Kiss Me
20" Star
A

Kiss Me
20" Star
C

Kiss Me
20" Star
B

Place on fold or trace full-size pattern.

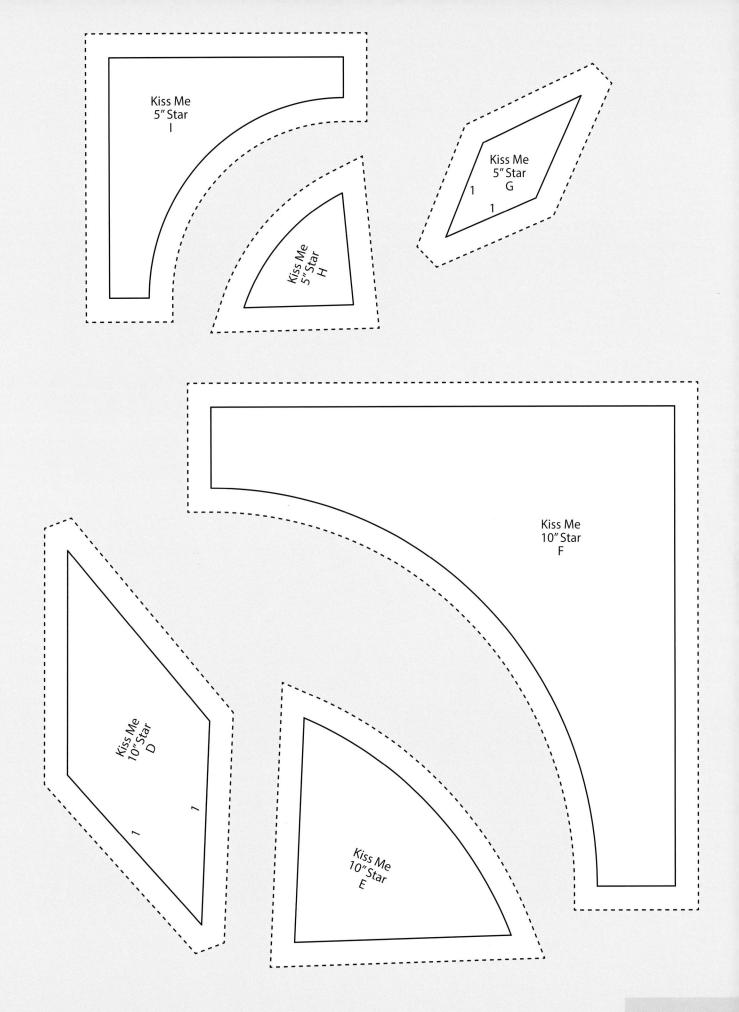

Kiss Me
5" Star
I

Kiss Me
5" Star
G

1
1

Kiss Me
5" Star
H

Kiss Me
10" Star
F

Kiss Me
10" Star
D

1
1

Kiss Me
10" Star
E

LITTLE BLACK DRESS

Every girl needs a little black dress. This would look fabulous on you, in dark blue and striking black prints, with sharp light neutrals for the bling.

Little Black Dress is made using a combination of paper piecing (foundation piecing) and templates.

MATERIALS

Assorted neutral prints: 9 fat quarters (2¼ yards total) for blocks

Assorted black and blue prints: 18 fat quarters (4½ yards total) for blocks

Black print 1: ⅝ yard for border 2

Neutral print: ¾ yard for border 2

Black print 2: 1 yard for border 1 and binding

Backing: 4 yards

Batting: 69″ × 77″

CUTTING

Use *Little Black Dress* foundation patterns A and B (page 41) to make the blocks. Use border patterns E–G (pages 39–41) to make templates E–G. For more information, review Paper Piecing (page 11) and Working with Templates (page 8).

NOTE

The cutting measurements for the foundation pieces A, B, C, and D are for rough-cuts. The measurements aren't meant to be exact, only to provide smaller pieces to work with and to help the fabric go as far as possible.

Assorted neutral prints

• Cut 38 strips 2½″ × 22″; subcut 224 rectangles 2½″ × 3½″ for A1 and B1.

• Cut 16 strips 3″ × 22″; subcut 112 squares 3″ × 3″; subcut once diagonally for 224 A3 and B3 triangles.

Assorted black and blue prints

• Cut 28 strips 4½″ × 22″; subcut 224 rectangles 4½″ × 2½″ for A2 and B2.

• Cut 75 strips 2½″ × 22″; subcut 224 rectangles 2½″ × 6½″ for A4 and A5.

Black print 1

• Cut 5 strips 2⅞″ × width of fabric; subcut 30 E pieces using template E.

• Cut 1 strip 3″ × width of fabric, subcut 4 corner squares 3″ × 3″.

Neutral print

• Cut 9 strips 2″ × width of fabric; subcut 52 F pieces using template F.

• Cut 1 strip 2½″ × width of fabric; fold strip in half crosswise and subcut 8 pieces using template G. The second layer will be 8 G-reverse pieces.

Black print 2

• Cut 7 strips 1½″ × width of fabric for border 1.

• Cut 8 strips 2¼″ × width of fabric for binding.

Construction

For information on the paper-piecing method I've used, see Paper Piecing (page 11).

BLOCK ASSEMBLY

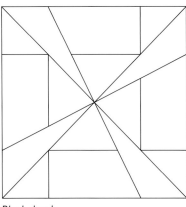

Block sketch

Section A

1. Cut the paper pattern apart into sections A and B, about ¼˝ outside the dashed line.

2. Sew A1 to A2, stitching along the solid line between A1 and A2.

3. Trim the seam and press it toward A2.

4. Add A3, A4, and A5, in order. Trim the seams and press between each piece.

5. Repeat Steps 1–4 to make 112 section A units.

Section B

1. Sew B1 to B2, stitching along the solid line between B1 and B2, as for section A.

2. Trim the seam and press it toward B2.

3. Add B3. Trim the seam and press it toward B3.

4. Repeat Steps 1–3 to make 112 section B units.

Finishing the Block

TIP

When joining sections, it is necessary to stitch through several layers of paper and fabric. A sharp needle really helps with this.

1. Stitch a section A piece to a section B piece. Press the seam toward section B.

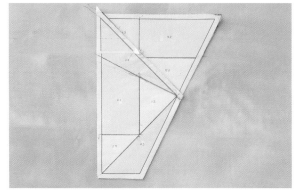

Stitch section A to section B.

2. Repeat Step 1 to make 112 half-blocks.

3. Sew the half-blocks together to make 56 blocks.

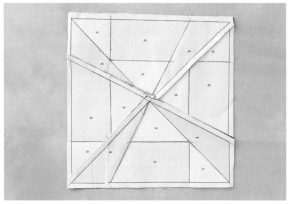

Join the half-blocks to make a block.

4. Remove the paper backing and press each block well, using a starch alternative.

Block assembly

ASSEMBLING THE QUILT TOP

1. Referring to the quilt assembly diagram (page 40), lay the blocks out in 8 rows of 7 blocks each.

2. Sew the blocks together into rows. Do not press until each row is complete.

3. Press the seams of the odd rows (1, 3, 5, and 7) to the right, and press the seams of the even rows (2, 4, 6, and 8) to the left.

TIP

The seam between these blocks can be bulky. A starch alternative will help to alleviate pressing issues.

4. Stitch the rows together, pinning the seams for accuracy. Because the odd row seams were pressed to the right and the even row seams to the left, the seams should nestle nicely.

5. Press all row seams in one direction, either up or down.

BORDER 1

For how to add border 1, see Measuring and Cutting Plain Borders (page 12).

BORDER 2

NOTE

For this border, we'll be switching from paper piecing to templates. For how to make and use templates, see Working with Templates (page 8).

1. Stitch an E piece to opposite sides of an F piece, as shown. Press the seams in one direction, either up or down.

Stitch E to F.

2. Repeat Step 1 to make a total of 22 E/F/E units.

3. Stitch a G piece, a G-reverse piece, and an E piece to an F piece, as shown, to make an end unit. Press all seams in the same direction.

4. Repeat Step 3 to make a total of 8 end units.

Make 8 end units.

5. Stitch 5 E/F/E units and 2 end units together to make the top border. Press all seams in the same direction. Repeat to make the bottom border.

6. Repeat Step 5 with 6 E/F/E units to make 2 side borders.

7. Stitch the 3″ × 3″ squares to each end of the side borders. Press the seams toward the squares.

8. Stitch the 2 shorter borders to the top and bottom of the quilt. Press toward border 1.

9. Stitch the 2 longer borders to the sides of the quilt. Press toward border 1.

FINISHING

1. Cut the backing fabric in half to make 2 sections 40″ × 72″.

2. Cut off the selvages and stitch the sections together along a 72″ side, using a ½″ seam allowance.

3. Layer, baste, quilt, and bind as desired.

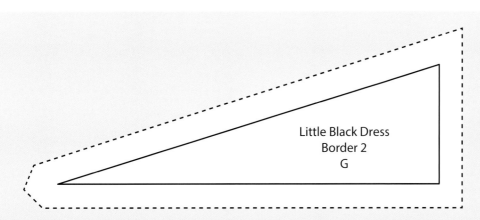

Little Black Dress
Border 2
G

Quilt assembly

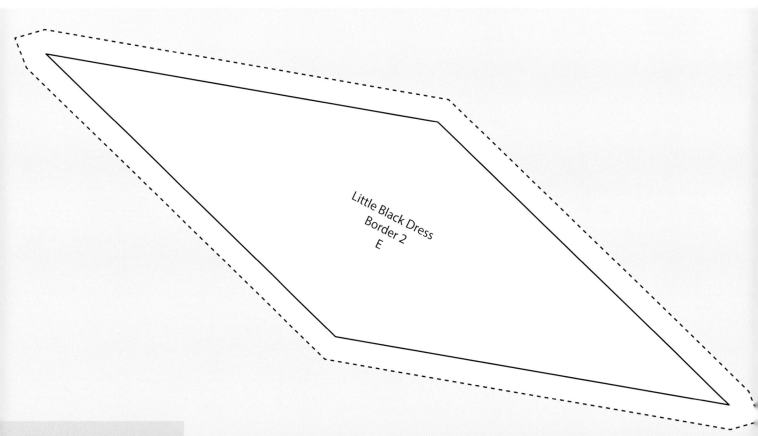

Little Black Dress
Border 2
E

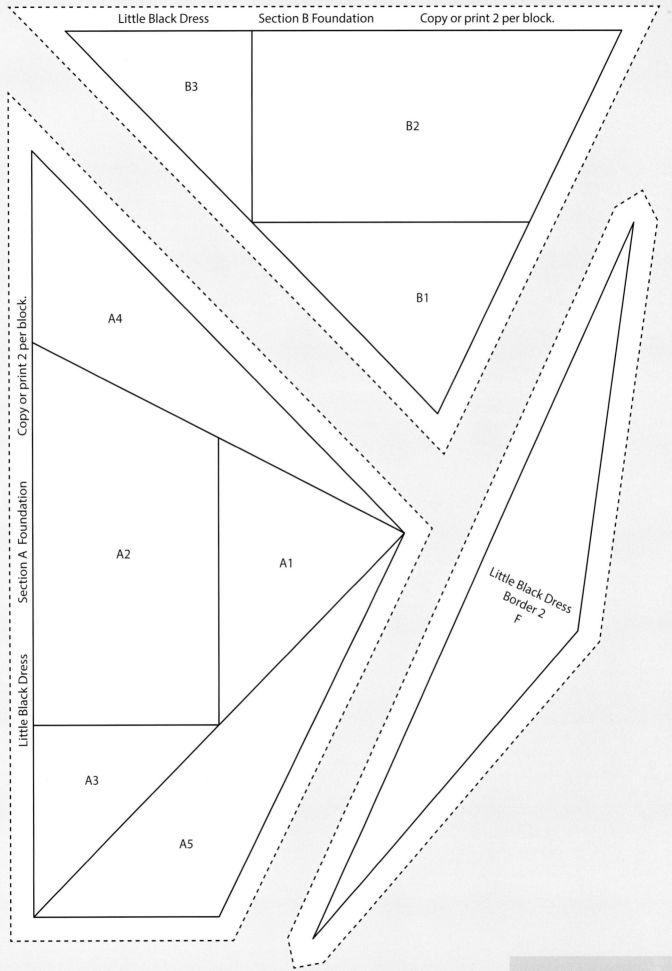

Little Black Dress   Section B Foundation   Copy or print 2 per block.

B3

B2

B1

Copy or print 2 per block.

Section A Foundation

Little Black Dress

A4

A2   A1

A3

A5

Little Black Dress
Border 2
F

MAD HOUSEWIFE

FINISHED BLOCK: 8″ × 8″

FINISHED QUILT: 75″ × 75″

LEVEL: Intermediate

Have you ever seen a woman running in four directions at once? I certainly have. In fact I've been her many times myself. This is my ode to that overworked mom chasing down her toddler in the grocery store. Make her a quilt, won't you? I used prints in brown, blue, sassy double-pink, and cheddar.

NOTE
Double-pink prints

What are "double-pink" prints? Quilt historian and designer Barbara Brackman, in her book *Making History: Quilts and Fabric from 1890 to 1970*, tells us that double-pink prints, described in color as "cinnamon," "strawberry," or "bubble-gum" pink, were actually the result of a technique in which two or more shades of pink were dyed on top of each other, probably because dyers were "unable to attain colorfast plain pastels until after 1910 or so." Whatever the reason, the results are stunning—double-pink prints are among my favorites, and I use them often!

I love fat quarters and, with the exception of the outer border and binding, I've used nothing but in this quilt. Fat quarters are the most economical way to collect a wide variety of fabrics. They lend this quilt its scrappy look. You could put a damper on too much scrappy madness by using one fabric for each color in each block.

Mad Housewife is made up of two different block colorings (brown and blue), for a total of 81 blocks.

MATERIALS

Assorted brown prints: 5 fat quarters (1¼ yards total) for blocks

Assorted blue prints: 4 fat quarters (1 yard total) for blocks

Assorted neutral prints: 14 fat quarters (3½ yards total) for blocks

Assorted double-pink prints: 5 fat quarters (1¼ yards total) for blocks

Assorted cheddar prints: 5 fat quarters (1¼ yards total) for blocks

Soft brown print: 1⅛ yards for border and binding

Backing: 4½ yards

Batting: 81″ × 81″

CUTTING

Cutting instructions for brown, blue, and neutral fabrics call for 22″ strips, because I've used fat quarters. The 22″ measurement is approximate, based on the typical fat quarter. There's no need to recut the strips to exactly 22″. Just use the length of the fat quarter.

Assorted brown prints

- Cut 17 strips 3⅞″ × 22″; subcut 82 squares 3⅞″ × 3⅞″; subcut once diagonally to yield 164 A triangles.

Assorted blue prints

- Cut 16 strips 3⅞″ × 22″; subcut 80 squares 3⅞″ × 3⅞″; subcut once diagonally to yield 160 A triangles.

Assorted neutral prints

NOTE

In each block of my quilt, I matched the B and E pieces. If you wish to do the same, cut sets of 4 of each piece from the same fabric.

- Cut 33 strips 3⅞″ × 22″; subcut 162 squares 3⅞″ × 3⅞″; subcut once diagonally to yield 324 B triangles.

- Cut 27 strips 3¼″ × 22″; subcut 162 squares 3¼″ × 3¼″; subcut once diagonally to yield 324 E triangles.

Assorted double-pink prints

Pay particular attention to the cutting instructions for the pinks and cheddars, as the pieces are directional. Unlike for nondirectional cutting, you'll have to sort through and turn all fabric pieces right side up before the final step.

- Cut 21 strips 1⅞″ × 22″; subcut 82 rectangles 1⅞″ × 4⅝″.
  Sort through and place all rectangles horizontally and right side up on cutting mat; subcut once diagonally from *bottom left corner to top right corner* to yield 164 C triangles for 41 brown blocks.

Directional cutting for the brown blocks

- Cut 20 strips 1⅞″ × 22″; subcut 80 rectangles 1⅞″ × 4⅝″.
  Sort through and place all rectangles horizontally and right side up on cutting mat; subcut once diagonally from *bottom right corner to top left corner* to yield 164 C triangles for 40 blue blocks.

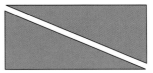

Directional cutting for the blue blocks

Assorted cheddar prints

- Cut 21 strips 1⅞″ × 22″; subcut 82 rectangles 1⅞″ × 4⅝″.
  Sort through and place all rectangles horizontally and right side up on cutting mat; subcut once diagonally from *bottom right corner to top left corner* to yield 164 D triangles for 41 brown blocks.

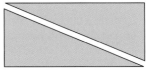

Directional cutting for the brown blocks

- Cut 20 strips 1⅞″ × 22″; subcut 80 rectangles 1⅞″ × 4⅝″.
  Sort through and place all rectangles horizontally and right side up on cutting mat; subcut once diagonally from *bottom left corner to top right corner* to yield 164 D triangles for 40 blue blocks.

Directional cutting for the blue blocks

Soft brown print

- Cut 8 strips 2″ × width of fabric for border.

- Cut 9 strips 2¼″ × width of fabric for binding.

Construction

Scant ¼″ seams are very important when working with triangles and other fine pieces. For more on sewing a scant ¼″ seam allowance, see Scant ¼″ Seams (page 7).

BLOCK ASSEMBLY

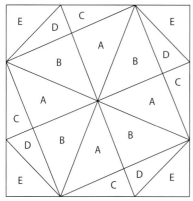

Block sketch

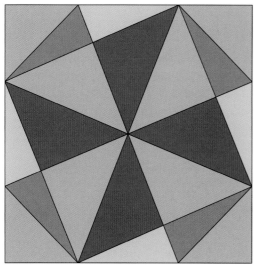

Brown block

Making the Pinwheels

For the crucial step of squaring the blocks, see Squaring Blocks (page 7).

1. Stitch an A triangle to a B triangle to make a half-square triangle. Press the seam toward the brown A triangle.

2. Repeat to make 4 A/B half-square triangles.

3. Square the half-square triangles to 3½″ × 3½″.

TIP

Arrange the half-square triangles into a pinwheel formation (see the block sketch, at left). I find it's easy to get these going the wrong direction, but laying them out keeps things from getting confusing.

4. Stitch the top 2 half-square triangles together. Press the seam toward the brown print.

5. Stitch the bottom 2 half-square triangles together. Press the seam toward the brown print.

6. Join the top and bottom halves to create the pinwheel. Press the joining seam to either side.

Adding the Double-Pink and Cheddar Triangles

1. Stitch a pink C triangle to a cheddar D triangle along the short side. Press the seam toward triangle C.

Stitch C to D for the brown blocks.

NOTE

As you'll see, the placement of the C and D triangles in the blocks determines which way the blocks tilt in the quilt.

2. Repeat to yield 4 C/D triangle units.

FINISHING THE BLOCK

Brown Block Assembly

1. Stitch a C/D unit to 1 side of the pinwheel block.

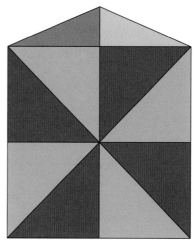

Stitch C/D to the pinwheel.

Because we pressed the pinwheel seams toward the brown print and the pink/cheddar triangle unit seams toward the pink print, the seams should nestle perfectly together.

2. Repeat 3 times so that each side of the pinwheel block is finished with a C/D triangle unit. Press toward the C/D units.

3. Stitch a neutral E triangle to a pink C triangle, ensuring that the E triangle is centered on the C triangle. Press the seam toward triangle E.

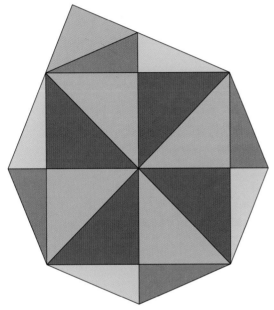

Finish with E patches.

4. Repeat 3 times so that each side of the pinwheel block is finished with an E triangle. Press well.

5. Repeat to make 41 brown blocks.

Blue Block Assembly

1. Follow the instructions for Making the Pinwheels, Steps 1–6 (page 45), using the blue and cream prints. Make 40.

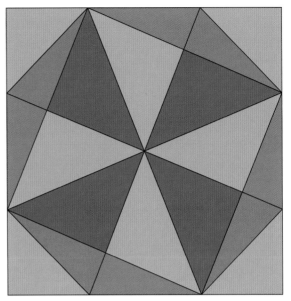

Blue block

2. Stitch a C triangle to a D triangle along the short side. *Note that the C and D placement is reversed for the blue blocks.* Press the seam toward triangle C.

3. Repeat to yield 4 C/D units.

4. Stitch a C/D unit to 1 side of the blue pinwheel block.

5. Repeat 3 times so that each side of the pinwheel block is finished with a C/D unit. Press the seams toward the C/D units.

6. Stitch an E triangle to a C triangle, ensuring that the E triangle is centered on the C triangle. Press toward triangle E.

7. Repeat 3 times so that each side of the pinwheel block is finished with an E triangle. Press well.

ASSEMBLING THE QUILT TOP

1. Referring to the quilt assembly diagram, sew the blocks into 9 rows of 9 blocks each, beginning and ending with a brown block. Note the orientation of each block within the row; the brown and blue blocks each tilt a different way. Do not press until each row is complete.

2. Press the seams of the odd rows (1, 3, 5, 7, and 9) to the right, and press the seams of the even rows (2, 4, 6, and 8) to the left. *The seam between these blocks can be bulky. A starch alternative will help to alleviate pressing issues.*

3. Sew the rows together, pinning the seams for accuracy. Because the odd row seams were pressed to the right and the even row seams to the left, the seams should nestle nicely together. Press all row seams in one direction, either up or down.

BORDER

For how to add the plain border, see Measuring and Cutting Plain Borders (page 12).

FINISHING

1. Cut the backing fabric in half to make 2 sections 40″ × 81″.

2. Cut off the selvages and stitch the sections together along an 81″ side, using a ½″ seam allowance.

3. Layer, baste, quilt, and bind as desired.

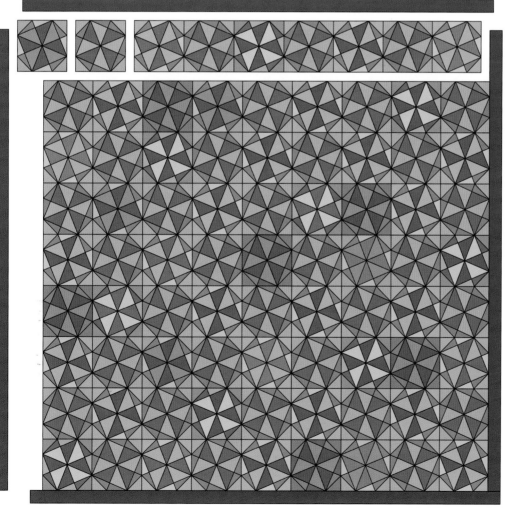

Quilt assembly

Peppá

FINISHED BLOCK: 8½″ × 8½″

FINISHED QUILT: 68″ × 68″

LEVEL: Beginner+

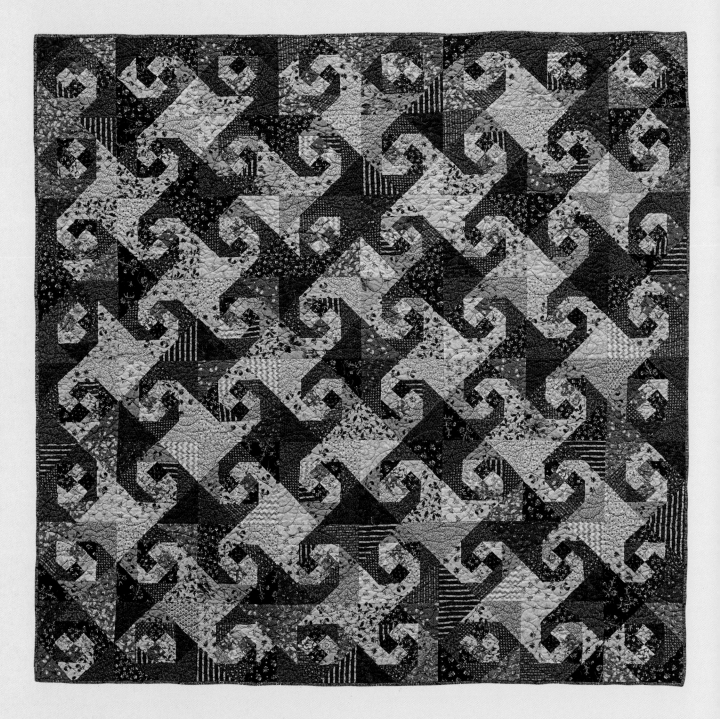

Small, sweet, and sassy—just like a peppermint. Make this quilt in hot pinks and yummy chocolate-brown prints. I added a binding of blue just to be cheeky.

Peppá is made up of four different block colorings, for a total of 64 blocks.

MATERIALS

Assorted dark pink and brown prints:
14 fat quarters (3½ yards total) for blocks

Assorted light- to medium-value neutral prints:
13 fat quarters (2¾ yards total) for blocks

Soft blue print: ⅝ yard for binding

Backing: 4⅛ yards

Batting: 74″ × 74″

CUTTING

Assorted dark pink and brown prints
- Cut 20 strips 5½″ × 22″; subcut 80 squares 5½″ × 5½″; subcut once diagonally to yield 160 dark D triangles.

- Cut 10 strips 4¼″ × 22″; subcut 48 squares 4¼″ × 4¼″; subcut once diagonally to yield 96 dark C triangles.

- Cut 11 strips 3¼″ × 22″; subcut 66 squares 3¼″ × 3¼″; subcut once diagonally to yield 132 dark B triangles.

- Cut 13 strips 2″ × 22″ for dark A strips.

Assorted light to medium neutral prints
- Cut 12 strips 5½″ × 22″; subcut 48 squares 5½″ × 5½″; subcut once diagonally to yield 96 light D triangles.

- Cut 16 strips 4¼″ × 22″; subcut 80 squares 4¼″ × 4¼″; subcut once diagonally to yield 160 light C triangles.

- Cut 11 strips 3¼″ × 22″; subcut 62 squares 3¼″ × 3¼″; subcut once diagonally to yield 124 light B triangles.

- Cut 13 strips 2″ × 22″ for light A strips.

Soft blue print
- Cut 8 strips 2¼″ × width of fabric for binding.

Construction

BLOCK ASSEMBLY

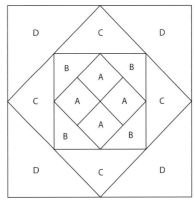

Block sketch

Making the Four-Patches

MAKING THE STRIP SETS

1. Create an A strip set by stitching a light 2″ × 22″ strip to a dark 2″ × 22″ strip. Press the seam toward the dark print. The strip sets should measure 3½″ wide.

2. Make 13 A light/dark strip sets.

3. Cut each strip set into 10 sections 2″ wide to yield 128 A sections.

JOINING THE STRIP SETS

1. Sew an A four-patch by joining 2 light/dark A sections. The seams should be opposing, making it easy to nestle them together. Press in either direction. The four-patch should measure 3½″ × 3½″.

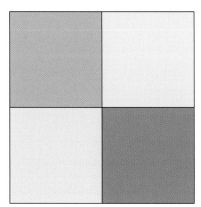

Four-patch

2. Repeat Step 1 to make 64 A four-patches.

Finishing the Block

NOTE

Peppá blocks are constructed by stitching 3 sets of triangles (B, C, and D) around an A four-patch, using partial seams. Pay particular attention when adding the triangles so that the light and dark triangles are in the correct position.

ADDING THE TRIANGLES

Follow these directions to add each set of triangles and square the block. The block illustrations show where to add lights and darks.

1. Fold a triangle in half to find the center of its long side. Match the triangle's center with the center of the side to which it will be stitched. Pin to secure.

2. Stitch the triangle (B, C, or D) to the four-patch.

3. Press the seam toward the triangle.

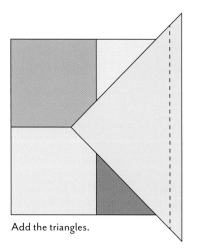

Add the triangles.

4. Repeat Steps 1–3 to add the remaining 3 triangles.

SQUARING THE BLOCK

Repeat this squaring-up step after each set of 4 triangles is added.

1. Lay the block in front of you on a cutting board.

2. Position a square ruler on the top of the block. (It's easiest to use a ruler that is just a bit larger than the block, but not too big.)

3. Adjust the placement of the ruler so that the ¼″ markings touch the four-patch or triangle point on the top and right side.

4. Trim the excess fabric at the ruler's edge, being very careful not to trim closer than ¼″ from the point.

5. Turn the block 180° and repeat, trimming the excess fabric on what is now the top and right side.

Square the Blocks

I've allowed a bit extra in the triangle measurements so that there will be enough excess to square the block to the exact measurement.

Here's what the blocks should measure after squaring:

- After adding B triangles: 4¾″ × 4¾″
- After adding C triangles: 6½″ × 6½″
- After adding D triangles: 9″ × 9″

6. Add the next set of 4 triangles to the four-patch blocks, noting where the lights and darks are positioned. Square the block, and then continue to add the C and D triangles, squaring between each set.

Block 1: Make 4 corner blocks.

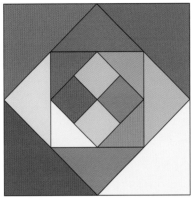

Block 2: Make 12 perimeter blocks.

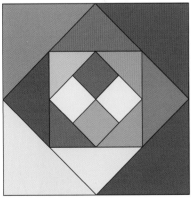

Block 3: Make 12 perimeter blocks.

Block 4: Make 36 interior blocks.

ASSEMBLING THE QUILT TOP

1. Referring to the quilt assembly diagram (page 52), assemble the blocks into 8 rows of 8 blocks each. Note the orientation of each block within the row; the lights and darks follow a very distinctive pattern.

2. Stitch the blocks together into rows. Do not press until each row is complete.

3. Press the joining seams of the odd rows (1, 3, 5, and 7) to the right, and press the joining seams of the even rows (2, 4, 6, and 8) to the left.

4. Sew the rows together, pinning the seams for accuracy. Because we pressed the odd row seams to the right and the even row seams to the left, the seams should nestle nicely together.

5. Press all row seams in one direction.

FINISHING

1. Cut the backing fabric in half to make 2 sections 40″ × 74″.

2. Cut off the selvages and stitch the sections together along a 74″ side, using a ½″ seam allowance.

3. Layer, baste, quilt, and bind as desired.

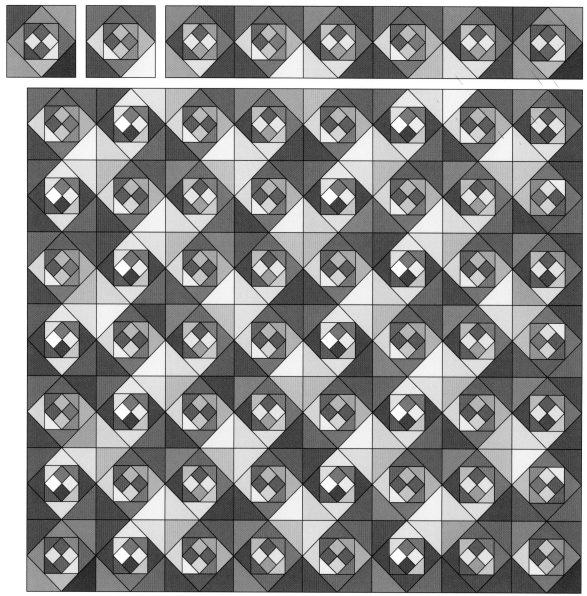

Quilt assembly

FINISHED BLOCK: 6″ × 6″

FINISHED QUILT: 69″ × 81″

LEVEL: Beginner+

POTION

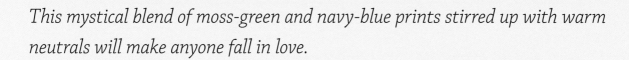

This mystical blend of moss-green and navy-blue prints stirred up with warm neutrals will make anyone fall in love.

This is a true scrap quilt made from my stash. I ended up with a colorway of greens and blues, but when choosing the fabrics, I was more interested in a fabric's value than its color. Once I had collected a good variety of scraps in all three values—light, medium, and dark—I was able to narrow down a colorway. It's a good way to create a scrap quilt; pieces you wouldn't imagine going together end up living happily ever after.

MATERIALS

Assorted light- and medium-value prints (moss greens, soft blues, medium grays, and warm neutrals): 11 fat quarters (2¾ yards total) for blocks

Assorted dark-value prints (navy blues, dark brown, and dark grays): 11 fat quarters (2¾ yards total) for blocks

Medium neutral print: ½ yard total for border 1

Dark blue print: 1½ yard for border 2 and binding

Backing: 5 yards

Batting: 75″ × 87″

CUTTING

NOTE

Directional Cutting

As with *Mad Housewife* (page 42) and *The Mister* (page 58), this quilt requires directional cutting. Pay particular attention to the cutting instructions for the B half-rectangles, as the patches are directional. Turn all rectangles right side up and horizontally, and cut them all the same direction.

Assorted light- and medium-value prints

- Cut 10 strips 3½″ × 22″; subcut 60 squares 3½″ × 3½″; subcut once diagonally to yield 120 A triangles.

- Cut 40 strips 3⅜″ × 22″; subcut 120 rectangles 3⅜″ × 6½″. Place each right side up and horizontally. Subcut once diagonally from *bottom right corner to upper left corner* to yield 240 B half-rectangles.

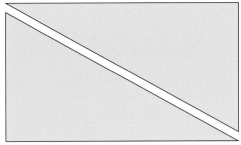
Cut B half-rectangles.

Assorted dark-value prints

- Cut 10 strips 3½″ × 22″; subcut 60 squares 3½″ × 3½″; subcut once diagonally to yield 120 A triangles.

- Cut 40 strips 3⅜″ × 22″; subcut 120 rectangles 3⅜″ × 6½″. Place each right side up and horizontally. Subcut once diagonally from *bottom right corner to upper left corner* to yield 240 B half-rectangles.

Medium neutral print

- Cut 8 strips 2″ × width of fabric for border 1.

Dark blue print

- Cut 8 strips 3½″ × width of fabric for border 2.

- Cut 9 strips 2¼″ × width of fabric for binding.

Construction

This block is constructed using partial seams, which are easy and fun—and another method to add to your repertoire.

BLOCK ASSEMBLY

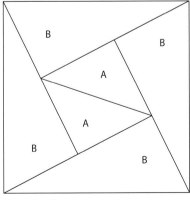
Block sketch

Making the Pinwheels

1. Stitch a light/medium A triangle to a dark A triangle to make a half-square triangle. Press toward the dark A triangle.

2. Repeat to make 120 A half-square triangle units.

3. Square the half-square triangle units to 3⅛″.

Adding the B Half-Rectangles

1. Place an A half-square triangle unit right side up, with the dark triangle at the upper left. Place a light B half-rectangle facedown, aligning the top and right sides to the light half of the half-square triangle unit.

2. Stitch the B half-rectangle to the half-square triangle along the right side, stopping about halfway down the half-square triangle. Finger-press the seam toward the A half-square triangle unit.

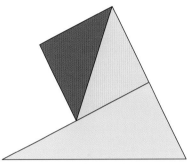
Add the light B half-rectangle.

NOTE
Partial Seams

Partial seams are used when other, adjacent seams must be stitched first before completing the seam. Stitch only halfway, and then stop and remove the unit from the machine. These seams can still be chain pieced; simply lift the presser foot and pull the unit out behind your machine a couple of inches, then begin stitching the next unit.

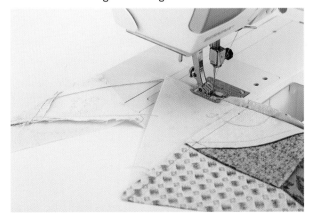
Chain piecing partial seams

3. Working in a counterclockwise direction, add the second light B half-rectangle and press the seam toward the A half-square triangle unit.

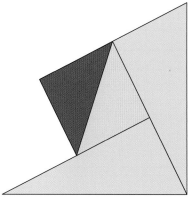

Add the second light B half-rectangle.

4. Add the dark B half-rectangle and press toward the B half-rectangle.

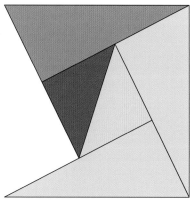

Add the dark B half-rectangle.

5. Add the second dark B half-rectangle and press toward the B half-rectangle.

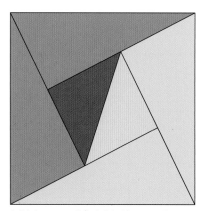

Add the second dark B half-rectangle.

FINISHING THE BLOCK

1. Finish the block by completing the partial seam sewn when adding the first B half-rectangle. Overlap 2 or 3 stitches to secure the partial seam.

2. Press well.

3. Repeat to make 120 blocks.

ASSEMBLING THE QUILT TOP

1. Referring to the quilt assembly diagram (next page), arrange the blocks in 12 rows of 10 blocks each. Note the orientation of each block within the row.

2. Stitch the blocks together into rows. Do not press until each row is complete.

3. Press the seams of the odd rows (1, 3, 5, 7, 9, and 11) to the right, and press the seams of the even rows (2, 4, 6, 8, 10, and 12) to the left.

4. Sew the rows together, pinning the seams for accuracy. Because the odd row seams were pressed to the right and the even row seams to the left, the seams should nestle nicely together.

5. Press all the row seams in one direction, either up or down.

BORDER 1 AND 2

To add the borders, see Measuring and Cutting Plain Borders (page 12).

FINISHING

1. Cut the backing fabric in half to make 2 sections 40″ × 90″.

2. Cut off the selvages and stitch the sections together along a 90″ side, using a ½″ seam allowance.

3. Layer, baste, quilt, and bind as desired.

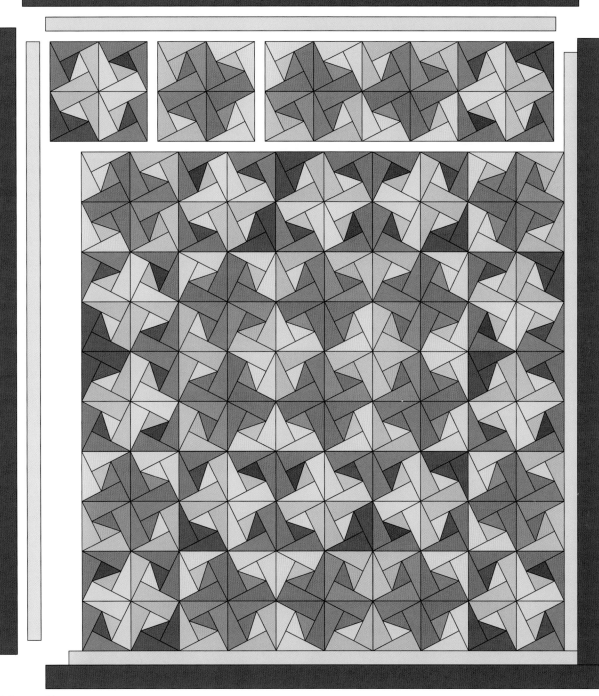

Quilt assembly

THE MISTER

FINISHED BLOCK: 10″ × 10″

FINISHED QUILT: 56″ × 86″

LEVEL: Intermediate

My own mister will, on occasion, curl up with a quilt for the game. This quilt is a great length; it covers his toes without being too bulky on the sides, and it fits his armchair perfectly.

NOTE Sports Fan?

Is your mister a sports fan, like mine? Make this quilt for him in his team colors, using the team's logo fabric for the borders.

MATERIALS

Assorted blue and purple prints: 13 fat quarters (3¼ yards total) for blocks

Assorted neutral prints: 13 fat quarters (3¼ yards total) for blocks

Dark gray print: ⅓ yard for top and bottom borders

Dark blue print: 1⅛ yards for side borders and binding

Backing: 5¼ yards

Batting: 62″ × 92″

CUTTING

Assorted blue and purple prints

- Cut 25 strips 2½″ × 22″; subcut 200 A squares 2½″ × 2½″.

- Cut 20 strips 2⅝″ × 22″; subcut 80 rectangles 2⅝″ × 5¼″. Place each right side up and horizontally. Subcut once diagonally from *bottom left corner to upper right corner* to yield 160 C half-rectangles.

Cut C half-rectangles.

TIP

Be sure to cut these as shown in the illustration (below left), as they are directional.

- Cut 10 strips 5¼″ × 22″; subcut 40 squares 5¼″ × 5¼″; subcut twice diagonally to yield 160 D triangles.

Assorted neutral prints

- Cut 23 strips 2⅞″ × 22″; subcut 160 squares 2⅞″ × 2⅞″; subcut once diagonally to yield 320 B triangles.

- Cut 20 strips 2⅝″ × 22″; subcut 80 rectangles 2⅝″ × 5¼″. Place each right side up and horizontally to subcut once diagonally from *bottom left corner to upper right corner* to yield 160 C half-rectangles.

- Cut 10 strips 5¼″ × 22″; subcut 40 squares 5¼″ × 5¼″; subcut twice diagonally to yield 160 D triangles.

Dark gray print for borders

- Cut 3 strips 3½″ × width of fabric for top and bottom borders.

Dark blue print

- Cut 5 strips 3½″ × width of fabric for side borders.

- Cut 8 strips 2¼″ × width of fabric for binding.

Construction

BLOCK ASSEMBLY

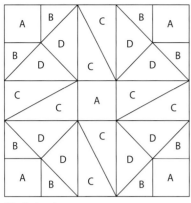

Block sketch

Making the Corner Units

1. Stitch a B triangle to an A square. Press toward the B triangle.

Stitch B to A.

2. Repeat to add a second B triangle to the adjacent side. Press toward the B triangle.

Add a second B triangle.

3. Stitch a blue/purple D triangle to a neutral D triangle along the short side. Note that the blue/purple triangle is always on the right when the pair is opened. Press to the blue/purple D triangle.

D/D triangle

4. Stitch the A/B unit to the D unit. Press toward the D unit.

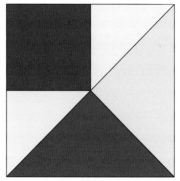

Finish the corner unit.

5. Repeat to make 160 corner units.

MAKING THE C UNITS

1. Stitch a blue/purple C triangle to a neutral C triangle. Press toward the blue/purple C triangle.

Stitch the C triangles.

2. Repeat to make 160 C units. Set aside 80 units for middle units and 80 units for the top and bottom units.

Making the Top and Bottom Units

1. Stitch a corner unit to each side of a C unit that was reserved (see previous page). Note the orientation of the corner units. Press toward the corner units.

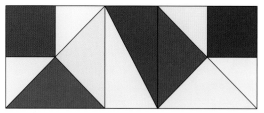

Stitch the corner units to a C unit.

2. Make 80 top and bottom units.

Making the Middle Units

1. Stitch a C unit to each side of an A square. Press toward the A square.

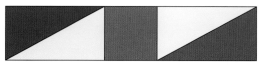

Stitch a C unit to an A square.

2. Make 40 middle units.

FINISHING THE BLOCK

1. Stitch a top and bottom unit to each side of a middle unit, matching the seams. Press toward the middle unit.

Block assembly

2. Repeat to make 40 blocks.

ASSEMBLING THE QUILT TOP

1. Referring to the quilt assembly diagram (page 62), arrange the blocks in 8 rows of 5 blocks each.

2. Stitch the blocks together into rows. Do not press until each row is complete.

3. Press the joining seams of the odd rows (1, 3, 5, and 7) to the right, and press the joining seams of the even rows (2, 4, 6, and 8) to the left.

4. Stitch the rows together, pinning the seams for accuracy.

5. Press all row seams in one direction, either up or down.

BORDER

See Measuring and Cutting Plain Borders (page 12) for adding plain borders. Add the top and bottom borders first and then the side borders.

FINISHING

1. Cut the backing fabric in half to make 2 sections 40˝ × 94˝.

2. Cut off the selvages and stitch the sections together along a 94˝ side, using a ½˝ seam allowance.

3. Layer, baste, quilt, and bind as desired.

Quilt assembly

FINISHED BLOCK: 9½″ × 9½″

FINISHED QUILT: 81″ × 90″

LEVEL: Intermediate

THE OATH

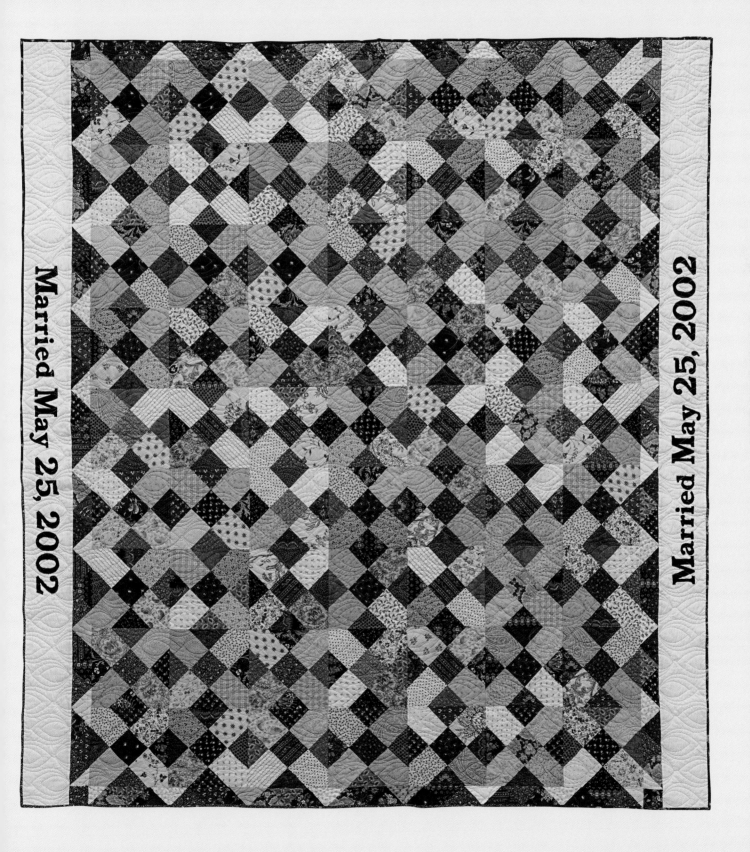

To all those who have served, protected, cherished, or made a Promise.

The Oath *is made up of 63 blocks and a wide, snowy-white border on just the sides, perfect for appliquéing service, wedding, or anniversary dates. I used a combination of soft, buttery neutrals and crisp florals for the lights to dress up the traditional red, white, and blue in this quilt.*

MATERIALS

Assorted light prints: 21 fat quarters (5¼ yards total) for blocks and border 1

Assorted red prints: 7 fat quarters (1¾ yards total) for blocks and border 1

Assorted blue prints: 8 fat quarters (2 yards total) for blocks and border 1

Light neutral print: 1⅛ yards for side borders

Red print: ¾ yard for binding

Backing: 7¼ yards

Batting: 87″ × 96″

CUTTING

Assorted neutral prints

- Cut 52 strips 6″ × 22″.

  Reserve 26 strips for A strips.

  From remaining 26 strips, subcut 126 A2 rectangles 6″ × 3⅞″.

- Cut 3 strips 6″ × 22″; subcut 7 squares 6″ × 6″; subcut twice diagonally to yield 28 D triangles.

- Cut 1 strip 3¼″ × 22″; subcut 4 squares 3¼″ × 3¼″; subcut once diagonally to yield 8 E triangles.

Assorted red prints

- Cut 6 strips 6″ × 22″; subcut 16 squares 6″ × 6″; subcut twice diagonally to yield 64 D triangles.

- Cut 13 strips 3⅞″ × 22″ for B strips.

- Cut 1 strip 2⅞″ × 22″; subcut 4 squares 2⅞″ × 2⅞″.

Assorted blue prints

- Cut 24 strips 6″ × 22″; subcut 71 squares 6″ × 6″; subcut twice diagonally to yield 252 C triangles and 32 D triangles.

TIP

Handle these triangles carefully, as the bias has now been exposed. I use a starch alternative when working with pieces that have an exposed bias edge. Giving the pieces a spritz and pressing before you cut them on the diagonal really helps keep their shape. You may find that if you've used the starch alternative lightly throughout, you may not need this step.

Light neutral print

- Cut 6 strips 5½″ × width of fabric.

Red print binding

- Cut 10 strips 2¼″ × width of fabric.

Construction

You may notice that I have used this block before, in the quilt called *Thistle* in my first book, *Fresh from the Prairies*. That's because I just love it! It's a simple block, but it's very versatile.

BLOCK ASSEMBLY

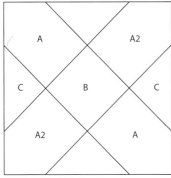

Block sketch

Making the Strip Sets

1. Create an A/B/A strip set by stitching a neutral A strip to each side of a red B strip.

2. Press the seams toward the neutral A strips.

TIP

When stitching strip sets, it's a good idea to set the seams by pressing before opening them. This helps take out any curve your machine may have introduced, especially in long seams.

3. Make 13 A/B/A strip sets.

A/B/A strip set

4. Cut each strip set into 5 A/B/A sections 3⅞″ wide, for a total of 63 A/B/A units.

NOTE

It's important to trim one end of the strip set before cutting it into sections, as the ends may not be square. Using the seamlines as guides, square up one end first.

Cut A/B/A units.

Making the End Units

1. Stitch a C triangle to each side of an A2 rectangle.

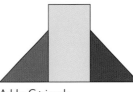

Add a C triangle.

2. Press toward the A2 rectangle.

3. Make 126 end units.

ASSEMBLING THE BLOCK

1. Gather together the A/B/A units and the end units. Referring to the block sketch, match and pin seams, and stitch an end unit to each side of an A/B/A unit. Press toward the end unit.

Stitch an end unit to each side of an A/B/A unit.

2. Square the blocks to 10″ × 10″ by trimming the A and A2 corners even with the edges of the C triangles and keeping the corners centered within the A and A2 pieces.

3. Make 63 blocks.

Square the block.

ASSEMBLING THE QUILT TOP

1. Referring to the quilt assembly diagram (next page), arrange the blocks in 7 rows of 9 blocks each.

2. Stitch the blocks together into rows. Do not press until each row is complete.

3. Press the seams of the odd rows (1, 3, 5, 7, and 9) to the right, and press the seams of the even rows (2, 4, 6, and 8) to the left. Using a starch alternative is helpful when pressing blocks with diagonal seams.

4. Stitch the rows together, pressing all row seams in the same direction, either up or down.

PIECED BORDER 1

Assembling the Pieced Border

This pieced border will be made in sections, which is one way to ensure that a long pieced border won't be handled too much and stretched during construction.

1. Trim the points of the D triangles ¼″, using a point trimmer.

2. Create a border section by stitching a red D triangle to each side of a blue D triangle.

Stitch red D triangles to each side of a blue D triangle.

3. Press in either direction, but press all seams in the same direction.

4. Make 32 red/blue/red units.

5. Stitch a neutral D triangle to each of 28 red/blue/red D units.

Stitch a D triangle to a red/blue/red unit.

6. Press all seams in the same direction.

7. Make 2 borders of 8 red/blue/red/neutral units and 2 borders of 6 red/blue/red/neutral units.

8. Stitch a neutral E triangle to the left end of each border section.

Stitching E triangles to border end units

9. Stitch a neutral E triangle to the right end of the last 4 red/blue/red D units, and then add to the right end of each border section.

10. Stitch a red 3″ × 3″ square to each end of the 2 side borders. Press toward the square.

BORDER 1

TIP Diagonal Seams

Because diagonal seams can be tricky to line up, I found it was really important to adjust and pin each seam carefully before sewing. How the seams line up is especially important for this border, as the triangles of the border finish the blocks.

1. Match and pin the seams of the top border to the quilt. Sew and press the seam toward the pieced border.

2. Repeat to add the bottom border.

3. Repeat to add the side borders.

BORDER 2

The Oath's wide side borders are meant to be embroidered or appliquéd with special dates, event remembrances, or messages. Kim Jamieson-Hirst did the beautiful lettering appliqué for this quilt. (See Acknowledgments, page 3, for more on Kim and her company.)

1. Trim the selvages on each end of the 5½″ border strips. Stitch the strips together to make one continuous strip, referring to Bias-Joined Seams (page 8).

2. Measure the length of the quilt through the center and at the sides. Average the 3 measurements and cut 2 strips to this length from the continuous strip constructed in Step 1.

3. Stitch a strip to one side of the quilt. Press toward the border.

4. Repeat to add the second strip to the remaining side. Press to the outer border.

FINISHING

1. Cut the backing fabric in half to make 3 sections 40˝ × 87˝.

2. Cut off the selvages and stitch the sections together along an 87˝ side, using a ½˝ seam allowance.

3. Layer, baste, quilt, and bind as desired.

NOTE Fabric Width
Most bolts of fabric are slightly wider than 40˝, so this backing will be just big enough. If you or your longarm quilter is concerned that this isn't enough fabric, a 108˝-wide quilt backing would be the solution.

Quilt assembly

THRIFT SHOP JUNKIE

FINISHED BLOCK:
6"' × 6"

FINISHED QUILT:
81" × 81"

LEVEL: Intermediate+

Have you ever seen a thrift shop junkie? She's the one who can rummage through all those haphazard racks and come out rocking a Nirvana T-shirt and vintage floral straight skirt. Two different blocks, each in three colorways, bring to life this quilt's busy, eccentric style. I've paired pieces from Barbara Brackman's fabric line Alice's Scrapbag with a few pieces from my stash.

For the colorful prints, I chose sunny avocado, vintage orange, and cherry red, and I looked especially for prints that seemed like they could someday make their way to a thrift shop.

MATERIALS

Assorted brown prints: 4¾ yards for blocks

Assorted colorful medium-value prints: 1⅝ yards for blocks

Assorted neutral prints: 2 yards for blocks

Large floral print: ⅞ yard for setting triangles and corners

Warm gold print: ½ yard for inner border

Blue print 1: 1 yard for top and bottom outer border and binding

Blue print 2: ⅜ yard for outer side borders

Backing: 7¼ yards

Batting: 87″ × 87″

CUTTING

Thrift Shop Junkie is made up of two different blocks—Whirlwind blocks and Hourglass blocks—each in three colorways, for a total of 145 blocks. You'll need to pay close attention when cutting to keep them organized. My mother, Louise Cutforth, who bravely volunteered to piece this quilt, put each set of pieces in a bowl with a sticky note identifying them. This prevented a nightmare of mixed-up pieces!

Assorted brown prints

- Cut 2 strips 3⅞″ × width of fabric; subcut 16 squares 3⅞″ × 3⅞″; subcut once diagonally to yield 32 D1 triangles.

- Cut 48 strips 2⅝″ × width of fabric; subcut 336 A rectangles 2⅝″ × 5¼″.

- Cut 13 strips 2″ × width of fabric for E2 strips.

Cutting continues …

CUTTING (continued)

Assorted colorful medium-value prints

- Cut 5 strips 4¼″ × width of fabric; subcut 40 squares 4¼″ × 4¼″; subcut twice diagonally to yield 160 B2 triangles.

- Cut 7 strips 3⅞″ × width of fabric; subcut 61 squares 3⅞″ × 3⅞″; subcut once diagonally to yield 122 C triangles.

Assorted neutral prints

- Cut 5 strips 4¼″ × width of fabric; subcut 44 squares 4¼″ × 4¼″; subcut twice diagonally to yield 176 B1 triangles.

- Cut 5 strips 3⅞″ × width of fabric; subcut 45 squares 3⅞″ × 3⅞″; subcut once diagonally to yield 90 D2 triangles.

- Cut 13 strips 2″ × width of fabric for E2 strips.

Large floral print

- Cut 2 strips 9¾″ × width of fabric; subcut 8 squares 9¾″ × 9¾″; subcut twice diagonally to yield 32 setting triangles.

- Cut 1 strip 5⅛″ × width of fabric; subcut 2 squares 5⅛″ × 5⅛″; subcut once diagonally to yield 4 corner triangles.

Warm gold print

- Cut 8 strips 1½″ × width of fabric for inner border.

Blue print 1

- Cut 5 strips 2″ × width of fabric for outer top and bottom border.

- Cut 9 strips 2¼″ × width of fabric for binding.

Blue print 2

- Cut 5 strips 2″ × width of fabric for outer side borders.

Construction

WHIRLWIND BLOCK ASSEMBLY

Divide the A and B pieces into these groups for the Whirlwind blocks.

	A rectangles	B1 triangles	B2 triangles
BLOCK 1	64	—	64
BLOCK 2	128	32	96
BLOCK 3	144	144	—

Block 1

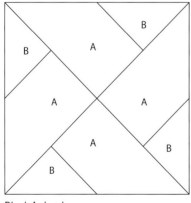

Block 1 sketch

1. Referring to the block 1 assembly diagram (next page), stitch a B2 triangle to the right side of an A rectangle. Press the seam toward B2. Repeat to make 4 A/B2 units.

2. Stitch an A/B2 unit to a second A/B2 unit to make a half-block. Press the seam toward A. Repeat to make a second half-block.

3. Matching and pinning seams, stitch the 2 half-blocks together. Press the seam in either direction.

4. Trim the rectangles to be even with the edges of the triangles. The block should measure 6½″ × 6½″.

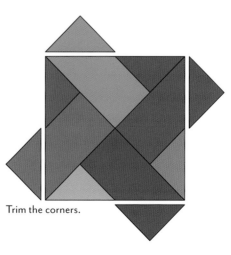

Trim the corners.

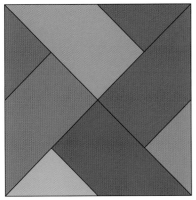

Block 1 assembly

5. Repeat Steps 1–4 to make 16 blocks.

Block 2

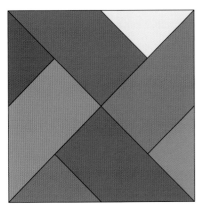

Block 2 assembly

1. Referring to the block 2 assembly diagram, stitch a B2 triangle to the right side of an A rectangle. Press the seam toward B2. Repeat to make 3 A/B2 units.

2. Stitch an A rectangle to a B1 triangle. Press the seam toward B1.

3. Stitch an A/B2 unit to an A/B1 unit to make a half-block. Press the seam toward the A/B1 unit.

4. Stitch an A/B2 unit to an A/B2 unit to make a half-block. Press the seam toward the A/B2 unit.

5. Matching and pinning seams, stitch the 2 half-blocks together. Press the seam in either direction.

6. Trim the rectangles to be even with the edges of the triangles. The block should measure 6½″ × 6½″.

7. Repeat Steps 1–6 to make 32 blocks.

Block 3

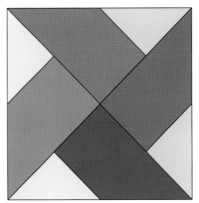

Block 3 assembly

1. Referring to the block 3 assembly diagram, stitch a B1 triangle to the right side of an A rectangle. Press the seam toward B1. Repeat to make 4 A/B1 units.

2. Stitch an A/B1 unit to a second A/B1 unit to make a half-block. Press the seam toward A. Repeat to make a second half-block.

3. Matching and pinning seams, stitch the 2 half-blocks together. Press the seam in either direction.

4. Trim the rectangles to be even with the edges of the triangles. The block should measure 6½″ × 6½″.

5. Repeat Steps 1–4 to make 36 blocks.

HOURGLASS BLOCK ASSEMBLY

Divide the D triangles into these groups for the Hourglass blocks.

	D1 triangle	D2 triangle
BLOCK 4	—	62
BLOCK 5	28	28
BLOCK 6	4	—

Making the Four-Patches

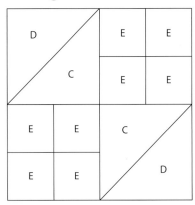

Hourglass block sketch

1. Create a strip set by stitching an E1 strip to an E2 strip. Press the seam toward E1. The strip set should measure 3½″ wide. Adjust your seam allowance if necessary.

2. Repeat to make 13 strips sets. Cut these into 2″ pairs for a total of 244 units.

3. Stitch pairs together to make a four-patch measuring 3½″ × 3½″. Press the seams in either direction.

4. Make 122 four-patches.

Making the Half-Square Triangles

1. Pair a C triangle with a D1 triangle, right sides together. Stitch together on the long side. Press the seam toward the C triangle.

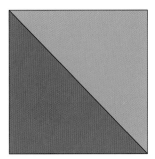

C/D1 half-square triangles

2. Repeat to make 32 C/D1 half-square triangles.

3. Pair a C triangle with a D2 triangle, right sides together. Stitch together on the long sides. Press toward the C triangle.

4. Repeat to make 90 C/D2 half-square triangles.

5. Referring to the block assembly diagrams, arrange the four-patch and half-square triangles into the following blocks.

BLOCK 4

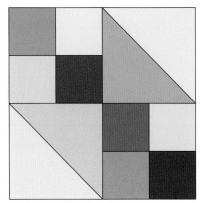

Block 4 assembly: Make 31.

BLOCK 5

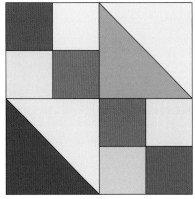

Block 5 assembly: Make 28.

BLOCK 6

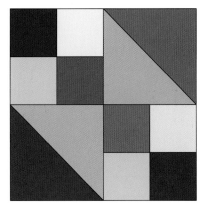

Block 6 assembly: Make 2.

ASSEMBLING THE QUILT TOP

1. Referring to the quilt assembly diagram, arrange the blocks in diagonal rows, noting the orientation of each block.

2. Position a large setting triangle at the ends of each row.

3. Matching and pinning seams, stitch the blocks together into rows. Do not press until each row is complete.

4. Press the seams of the odd rows (1, 3, 5, and so on) to the right, and press the seams of the even rows (2, 4, 6, and so on) to the left.

5. Match and pin seams, join the rows together to make the quilt center. Press the seams of the joining rows in either direction.

5. To add the corner triangles, first fold the corner triangles in half and finger-press or pin to mark the center. Match the fold with the center of each of the four corner blocks. Pin and stitch in place. Press toward the corners.

Borders

To add the inner and outer borders, see Measuring and Cutting Plain Borders (page 12).

FINISHING

1. Cut the backing fabric in thirds to make 3 sections 40″ × 87″.

2. Cut off the selvages and stitch the sections together along an 87″ side, using a ½″ seam allowance.

3. Layer, baste, quilt, and bind as desired.

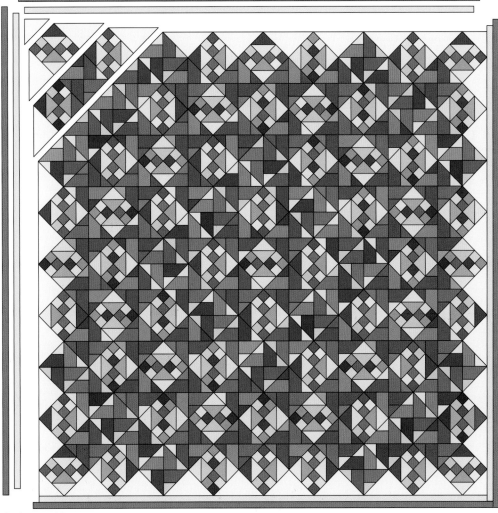

Quilt assembly

TWENTY-FIVE

FINISHED BLOCK: 9″ × 9″

FINISHED QUILT: 53″ × 53″

LEVEL: Intermediate +

When you're 25, everything is bright and golden and full of promise—until it's rent day once again. Make this cheery quilt for the 25-year-old in your life—in sunny yellow, soft gold, and olive prints (and a bit of gray for the rent days).

To achieve this quilt's soft and scrappy look, cut each shape from a variety of the prints listed. For instance, the A triangles require four strips cut from each color. Cut each strip from a different print.

Although I used fat quarters for the blocks, I used only one print for the light triangles in border 1.

MATERIALS

Assorted soft gold and olive prints: 12 fat quarters (3 yards total) for blocks and border 1

Assorted sunny yellow prints: 4 fat quarters (1 yard total) for blocks

Assorted light neutral prints: 2 fat quarters (½ yard total) for blocks

Assorted soft gray prints: 3 fat quarters (¾ yard total) for blocks

Light neutral print: ¾ yard for border 1

Warm gold print: 1 yard for border 2 and binding

Backing: 3⅓ yards

Batting: 59″ × 59″

CUTTING

Use *Twenty-Five* patterns B–G (page 79) to make templates B–G. For information on making and using templates, review Working with Templates (page 8).

Assorted soft gold and olive prints

- Cut 4 strips 3⅞″ × 22″; subcut 20 squares 3⅞″ × 3⅞″; subcut twice diagonally to yield 80 A triangles.

- Cut 100 B triangles.
- Cut 100 F triangles.
- Cut 50 C pieces.
- Cut 20 G triangles.
- Cut 50 D triangles.

Assorted sunny yellow prints

- Cut 50 C pieces.
- Cut 50 D triangles.

Assorted light neutral prints

- Cut 5 strips 3⅞″ × 22″; subcut 25 squares 3⅞″ × 3⅞″; subcut twice diagonally to yield 100 A triangles.

Assorted soft gray prints

- Cut 1 strip 3⅞″ × 22″; subcut 5 squares 3⅞″ × 3⅞″; subcut twice diagonally to yield 20 A triangles.

- Cut 100 E triangles.

Cutting continues…

CUTTING (continued)

Light neutral print

- Cut 16 G triangles.

- Cut 4 F triangles and 4 F-reverse triangles.

- Cut 1 strip 2⅜″ × width of fabric; subcut 4 squares 2⅜″ × 2⅜″.

Warm gold print

- Cut 6 strips 2½″ × width of fabric for border 2.

- Cut 6 strips 2¼″ × width of fabric for binding.

Construction

BLOCK ASSEMBLY

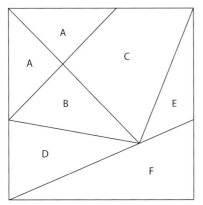

Mini-block sketch

Making the Mini-Blocks

TIP

The trick to stitching these pieces is to match the edges, including the rounded ends you carefully cut. This will take the guesswork out of where the pieces are stitched in relation to each other.

1. Stitch a neutral A to a soft gold A along one short side. Press toward the gold A.

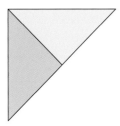

Stitch the A triangles.

2. Stitch a soft gold B to a sunny yellow C. See the mini-block sketch for positioning. It's easy to get these pieces turned around (especially when working with batiks), so make sure that yours match the sketch. Press the seam toward C.

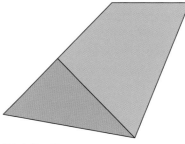

Stitch B to C.

3. Matching and pinning the seam, stitch an A unit to a B/C unit. Press the seam toward the A unit.

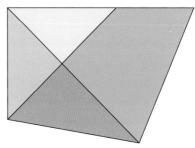

Stitch an A unit to a B/C unit.

4. Stitch a sunny yellow D to the B side of this unit. Again, be careful to position D properly. Press the seam toward the gold B fabric.

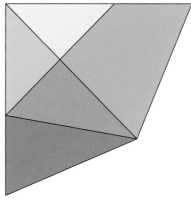

Stitch D to the B side of the unit.

5. Stitch a soft gray E to the C side of this unit. Press to the gray E fabric.

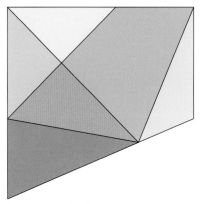

Stitch an E to the C side of the unit.

6. Stitch a gold F to the D and E side of the unit. Press the seam toward the gold F fabric.

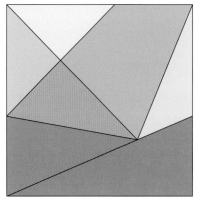

Stitch F to the D and E side of the unit.

NOTE
Chain Piecing the Mini Blocks

It's very easy to chain piece these blocks. After you've made one or two blocks and are happy with how they go together, you can begin to chain piece. Feed the pieces through just as you would regular pieces, using a scant ¼˝ seam. Sometimes you have to help guide irregularly shaped pieces to get them started. I use an awl for this, as I have learned from several piecing gurus.

Joining the Mini-Blocks

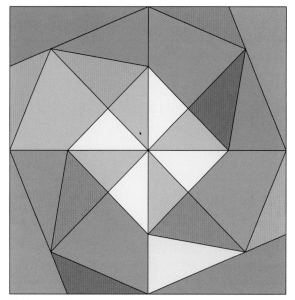

Block assembly

1. Arrange 4 mini-blocks as shown in the block assembly diagram.

2. Stitch each pair together. Press the seams in opposite directions.

3. Stitch the 2 pairs together.

4. Press the seams toward either side. Using a starch alternative, press the block well.

NOTE
Finished Versus Unfinished

References to finished and unfinished block sizes can be confusing. The finished size generally refers to the measurement of the block once it is placed with its fellows in the quilt, but on occasion, the word *finished* just means "complete." I use the word *finished* to mean the finished measurement after the block is complete. So this block, unfinished right now, should measure 9½˝ × 9½˝. Once it is stitched with other blocks all around it, it will measure 9˝ × 9˝.

5. Repeat Steps 1–4 to make 25 blocks.

ASSEMBLING THE QUILT TOP

1. Referring to the quilt assembly diagram (below right), arrange the blocks in 5 rows of 5 blocks each.

2. Stitch the blocks into rows. Do not press until each row is complete. Press the joining seams of the odd rows (1, 3, and 5) to the right, and press the joining seams of the even rows (2 and 4) to the left.

TIP

The seams between these blocks can be bulky. Pressing with starch alternative will help to alleviate pressing issues.

3. Sew the rows together, pinning the seams for accuracy. Because the odd row seams were pressed to the right and the even row seams to the left, the seams should nestle nicely together. Press all row seams in one direction, either up or down.

PIECED BORDER 1

1. Stitch a neutral G to a gold G on the short side, as shown. Press toward the neutral G fabric.

Stitch the G border pieces.

NOTE

When making borders from pieces with bias edges, it's important that you don't stretch the pieces while pressing and handling.

2. Continue to add neutral and gold G pieces to create a border that begins and ends with a gold G triangle. There will be 5 gold and 4 neutral pieces.

3. Stitch an F half-rectangle to each end of the border. Press toward the neutral F fabric.

4. Repeat to make 4 borders.

5. Match and pin the seams of the top border to the quilt and sew. Press the seam toward the quilt top.

6. Repeat Step 5 to add the bottom border.

7. Stitch a 2⅜″ × 2⅜″ square to the ends of the 2 remaining borders. Press the seam toward the square.

8. Repeat Step 5 to add these borders to the side of the quilt.

BORDER 2

For adding plain borders, see Measuring and Cutting Plain Borders (page 12).

FINISHING

1. Cut the backing fabric in half to make 2 sections 40″ × 60″.

2. Cut off the selvages and stitch the sections together along the 60″ side, using a ½″ seam allowance.

3. Layer, baste, quilt, and bind as desired.

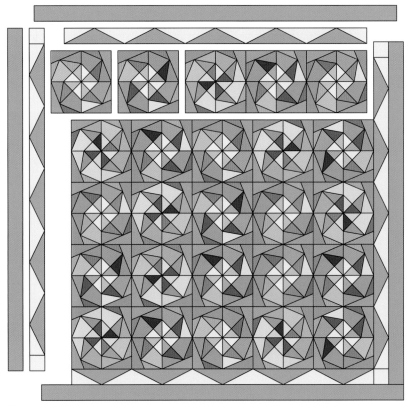

Quilt assembly

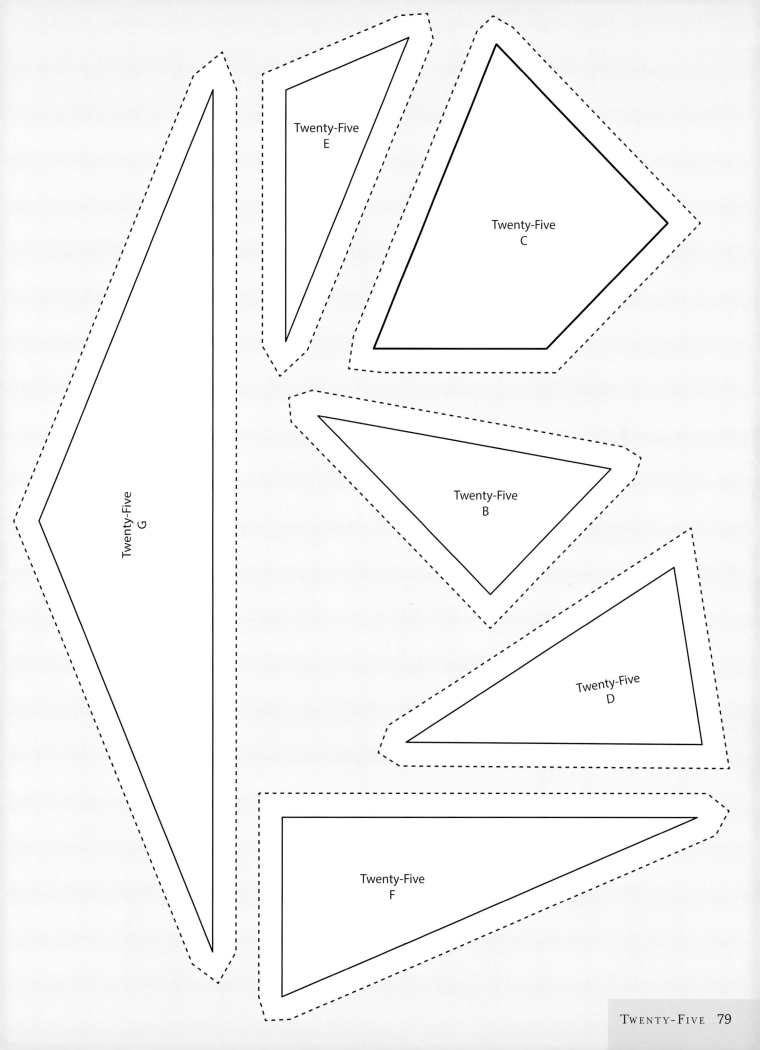

Twenty-Five
E

Twenty-Five
C

Twenty-Five
G

Twenty-Five
B

Twenty-Five
D

Twenty-Five
F

ABOUT THE AUTHOR

Devon Lavigne is a quiltmaker, author, and teacher. *Quilting Traditions* is her second book, and her designs have been published in several magazines, including *Fons & Porter*, *Primitive Quilts and Projects*, *Quilt Magazine*, and *Quilter's World*.

She lives with her husband and pups on ten acres in rural Drumheller, Canada, and recently welcomed her first grandbaby.

Also by Devon Lavigne:

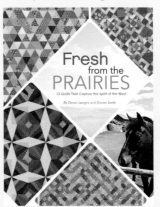

Want even more creative content?

Go to ctpub.com/offer

& sign up to receive our gift to you!

Make it, snap it, share it *using* #ctpublishing